The Book

of

MENTAL

TOUGHNESS

MANTRAS

Praise for

The Book of Mental Toughness Mantras

"The new Steve Chandler. Chris Dorris' new book *The Book of Mental Toughness Mantras* is like alchemy, turning base metals into gold. In a world of maximized word counts and complex theory in ever-increasing manuals, Chris brings a masterful clarity and ease to life through each magical reminder. Keep copies ready to read again on your bedside table, in your car, in your bathroom, on your coffee table, and give one to each of your best friends. The simple and colorful wisdom effortlessly revealed within this book will enhance your life, moment to moment."

Dr. Alan D. Thompson, AI Consultant at LifeArchitect.ai, co-author of *The Ultimate Coach*, Former Chairman for Mensa International (gifted families)

"There's some real Magic in these Mantras."

Jon Dorenbos, Keynote Speaker, AGT Finalist, fourteen-year NFL Player and two-time Pro-Bowler

"I love this book! Every day, our minds have the opportunity to spin out of control. We churn and burn in the whirlpool of stress, worry, catastrophizing, or a million other crazy-making emotions. This book is your life-jacket. Chris Dorris has the ability to make the profound simple by giving us all mantras where we can rest our thoughts. But it's more than that. The concepts in this book are thought-changing… actually, LIFE-CHANGING if we just set our minds on using them. Keep it by your desk and live one every day. I know from my own experience, you will see incredible results."

Alison "Doc Ali" Arnold, Ph.D., President, HeadGamesH2H: Emotional Agility

"This book represents Chris's core value—service. The lessons are deep and the application of them is easy. I reach out to Chris a lot, and I really appreciate how he uses these Mantras in our dialogues. The Mantras are tools that will benefit you enormously, if you will use them. I encourage you to absorb the wisdom! This is one of the best personal development books I've ever read."

Manisha Koirala, Bollywood actor, author of *Healed: How Cancer Gave Me a New Life*

"As a business leader, I fully comprehend the vital role of Emotional Mastery in creating success. The mantras that Chris includes in this book are brilliantly simple and magically practical tools for helping people keep their minds tuned to create excellence in all areas of their lives faster."

Garry Ridge, Chairman Emeritus WD-40 Company, The Culture Coach

The Book

of

MENTAL

TOUGHNESS

MANTRAS

Chris Dorris

Dedication

To my lifelong hero. My rock.
My perpetual source of unconditional support.
My big sis. Patty "V's Up!" Dorris Crenny.

Table of Contents

Foreword

Have you ever had someone say something to you, and as soon as the words were spoken you felt something shift inside you?

You remember the exact time and place these moments happened. Once the words left the person's lips they connected directly to your heart and every fiber of your being.

I've had several times in my life when this has occurred, and once in a while the impact has been so deep and powerful that it continues to reverberate in my spirit.

There's one particular time, fairly recently, where this happened and it had a profound impact. They were eight simple words, which might have easily been brushed over, but which I could not ignore:

"I did what I said I would do!"

These eight words had a transformative effect on my

life. From the moment I heard them, I felt a shift inside of me. Why? Was it the message? Was it the vibe I was getting? Was it the messenger?

All or none of the above?

We'll come back to that . . . For now, take a look at your life and hear these words through a new listening. A listening that is generous and heart-centered, and which hears the words as if they are coming from YOU.

"I do what I say I do!"

What could be possible for you if you lived a life where you said something and knew it would happen— not one time, but every time?

For instance, if you said, "I want to make my relationship stronger, more passionate and more loving"—and it happened, no matter what, because you said it would?

"I want to follow my dream and create a multi-million dollar business"—and it happened, no matter what, because you said it would?

"I want to take time to travel the world"—and it happened, no matter what, because of what you said?

"I want to _____."

Fill in the blank and imagine a life where creation is

literally on the tip of your tongue and in the actions that follow your words. You say it and you do it, no matter what.

You create a life where there are no longer reasons, circumstances or excuses that get in the way. A life where you see that nothing is more powerful, generative and certain than your word and your commitment to it.

A life as simple as one where every time you say you'll do something, it gets done!

Can you feel the power, freedom, self-expression and possibilities that would be created in your life? This life where your word (to yourself and others) literally creates the world you live in?

I remember the exact day when I heard the words, "I did what I said I would do," and experienced the power of just such a creation. It was one of those rare occasions where the message and the messenger were so aligned that you could feel it. It was so embedded in the delivery that you knew it could only come from one place—deep inside—and it was arrived at through profound inner work. It was one of those moments in life when a new possibility arose out of nothing—a true miracle in my awareness. In that moment I realized that the person standing in front of me had something I knew I wanted.

It was his delivery of the words, and most of all his way of Being, when he uttered the words, "I did what I said I would do," which pointed to a much bigger story. A story that my spirit could hear loud and clear, a story that transcended time, space and bullshit. It was a story about commitment, service, love and creativity. If you listened close enough it was also a story of pain, resilience, perseverance, and forgiveness. It was a story (hidden in an eight-word phrase) of Mental Toughness. I felt profound joy mixed with an honoring of what it had taken to get to that point for the person delivering the message.

That man is Chris Dorris.

"I did what I said I would do" was his response to an acknowledgement that I was giving him about the magnificence he had created in his own life and the lives of so many people around the planet. Chris is THE leader in Mental Toughness coaching and speaking around the world. His impact has had ripple effects in the world of pro sports, sales and business, and in the homes of everyday people who receive his daily doses of email wisdom.

Chris Dorris (CD) is the greatest creator of

community that I know—whether it's building a community of leaders in a company or connecting two strangers he knows should be connected. Or maybe it's his legendary Sunday Football get-togethers with his fellow Eagles fans. Chris brings people together in a special and unique way. And while he's known as the Mental Toughness guru, CD is much more than that. He is one of the most genuine and generous human beings on the planet, whose singular focus is to alter the lives of as many people as he can by upgrading their thoughts and actions.

What people don't know is that his "secret sauce" is the profound way he embodies loving service in all that he does. I've never met another human being who gives of himself through loving generosity more than Chris. He is also a straight-shooter from the east coast, and as a New Yorker I appreciate that, yet he is uniquely equipped to balance his straight talk with an open, generous and loving heart. This creates a range of emotional mastery that most people don't reach, one that allows him to be tough yet loving in all that he does.

He is the creator of #BDDOML, an acronym that stands for BEST DAMN DAY OF MY LIFE, which he repeats to himself and to anyone he encounters who asks him, "How are you doing?" And when CD replies, "This is the Best Damn Day of My Life," he means it! It's not just a catchy phrase. He has trained his mind to a point of mastery where every day he "creates the state" of that day being the best day of his life. This is just one of many examples of how CD actualizes what he's about to share with you in this book. What you are holding in your hands has the ability to upgrade your thoughts, emotions, behaviors and actions to the level of world-class performers around the world.

What you have in your hands is a masterpiece of mantras. These aren't mantras in the traditional sense. These aren't just cute phrases or affirmations that sound great but which have no impact. The book you are about to read has the ability to create a profound shift inside of you, like those eight words did in me that day. You'll see why in a moment. For now just know that what you are holding in your hands is pure alchemy.

"I did what I said I'd do!"

I've told you that when Chris said these words to me, we were looking around at everything he'd created in his life and in the lives of the people he serves all day, every day. We were celebrating his journey from South Jersey to a beautiful home in Chandler, Arizona, the community of friends who had become family, and most importantly how his life's work was evident in all the lives he touches.

None of this was by accident, I would learn. His was a life by design.

This vision and design weren't started by a grown man with a lot of resources. No, they were created by a sixteen-year-old boy growing up near the Jersey shore in the midst of confusion, chaos and darkness. A boy who had learned to navigate through significant trauma, suffering and violations of trust. A sixteen-year-old who by any stretch of the imagination could have taken a different road marked by anger, hurt and resentment—and because of what he endured, nobody would have blamed him. At age sixteen that young boy made a promise to himself, and that promise has positively impacted so many lives around the world.

His promise was, "I am going to do what I say I will do!"

"I am going to rise above the trauma, chaos and confusion in order to help others.

"I am going to feel, heal and deal in order to create a life that I love and show others that it's possible for them too.

"I am going to give hope to the hopeless, a voice to the voiceless and choices to the choiceless.

"That's what I am going to do, and I do what I say I do!"

That is who Chris Dorris is. A man who does what he says he will do. Every time!

After making that promise he dedicated the next thirty-seven years of his life to learning, studying and becoming the leader in Mental Toughness Training. He initially took to the streets of Atlantic City to bring that hope to people living with schizophrenia, working with the most vulnerable people whom others had given up on. Chris Dorris doesn't give up on people. He then took his passion to make a difference to Arizona State University, where his studies in biology, psychology and human behavior catapulted him into the role of Mental Toughness coach for the ASU Golf Team, and eventually into working with the greatest PGA Golfers in the world.

CD didn't stop there. When he realized that this work

could be taken off the golf course and into the companies and homes of leaders around the world, he did just that. He chose to make this work accessible to anyone who was ready to up-level their life. I myself use his Mental Toughness mantras in the work I do. I imagine if you're reading this that you might be one of those leaders, too— or you want to be—whether it's a leader in a company, in your home or in your community. We all have the capacity to use what's in this book to up-level our life and the lives of those around us.

You see, I can relate, and I know you can too. We've all had our versions of difficulty, suffering and feeling like there's no way out and nobody will understand. It took me years to figure out what CD was already aware of at the age of sixteen: the only way out is THROUGH. And his commitment to go through has resulted in the book that you have in your hands. This is the person you want to learn from—someone who walks his talk and about whom I can say his "audio matches his video." What he says and what he does are in perfect alignment.

The learnings CD brings to you in this this book are manifestations of the highest vibrations and teachings of Mental Toughness in the world. They will save you years of unnecessary dis-ease, suffering and complacency. *The Book of Mental Toughness Mantras* will uplift your mind, body and spirit in ways that will sometimes feel other-worldly. Why? Because these aren't just words in a book. They are embodiments of ideas from the minds of some of the greatest people in history, and they are used by the top performers in every industry. CD is the Jack Nicklaus of Mental Toughness, so if you're ready to learn, you might as well learn from the best.

Chris is the realest of the real deals. I've been around people who have talked a great game, but Chris lives it. He's studied with the most beloved and respected teachers, coaches and gurus in the world. He's learned from everyone, from the Dali Lama to Gurus in India, and he humbly brings his work to the world without bravado.

He has written this book for YOU. He's talking to and about you. The words will move you internally and catapult you into action externally.

One of the greatest miracles of my life was created based on this work. And you will start to see miracles in your own life immediately upon using what's in this book.

Foreword

This book will change your life.

Someone may ask you, "What is the point of Mental Toughness Training and mantras?"

I'll share some of CD's words on this:

"That's simple (and profound). We do the inner world work so that we are able to respond to all of life rapidly with grace, mastery, creativity, and enthusiasm. Mental Toughness Training involves strengthening our 'response-ability.' In other words, our ability to respond powerfully to all circumstances so that not only do we eliminate the unnecessary suffering we create for ourselves, but rather we create excellence faster and with less effort!

One of the most powerful ways to accomplish all of this is with the use of Mental Toughness Mantras—brief phrases that contain volumes of wisdom and that help us to elevate our states and create habitual, high-grade responses to ALL of life."

That's it!

Buckle up because your life is about to go from good to great! Or from already great to stratospheric!

Just because you've chosen to read this book. Because this is more than a book. These are words of transformation.

They represent what's possible for you: a life in which you can eliminate unnecessary suffering and create excellence faster and with less effort.

You're learning from the best, so strap in, buckle up and get ready for the most powerful, loving and transformational ride of your life.

Let's GOOOOOO!!!!

Devon Bandison
Go To Mind Coach, NBA

Introduction

In my work as a coach, speaker and author, I rely heavily on the value that mantras possess and the purposes that they serve. I think of mantras as mega-abbreviated, super-condensed versions of some of the most important lessons we would ever want to stay conscious of as we go through life.

Put another way, I read once that a mantra is a protector of the mind. I just love that definition—so let's go with it for this book.

For me, the shorter the mantra, the better. That way they're easier to remember. Especially if they rhyme. It isn't always easy to make them brief, and even more challenging to make them rhyme. But each of the mantras that I have chosen to include and elaborate upon in this book share a few common threads:

- They all relate to Mental Toughness

- They all contain volumes of wisdom
- They're all brief

Most of these mantras I've picked up along the way from someone whom I've studied. Some of them are my personal twists on ones I've learned. And a couple I've made up. They all serve as powerful reMINDers for us.

There is some overlap amongst them, and I see that as a great thing. And I ask you to see it the same way. A Master Carpenter has a massive toolbox full of tools that he uses to craft his amazing creations. And many of those tools are very similar and perform similar functions—but they aren't identical. He may, for example, have many types of saws: a miter saw, a table saw, a bow saw, hacksaw, chainsaw, jigsaw, etc. They all cut wood, but not in precisely the same ways. Each of them is perfect for a certain job.

Similarly, some of these mantras are similar in nature, but one may be perfect for a specific life circumstance whereas another might still get the job done, but perhaps not as effectively or as masterfully.

Ultimately, you'll decide which of these are useful for you, and in which circumstances. I'll do my best to elaborate upon them in ways that are relevant and impressionable for you.

But it will be up to you to determine what each one means to you. And the practice is to develop the habit of reciting these mantras to yourself throughout the day to remind yourself of how you prefer to interpret reality, how you want to feel from moment to moment, and finally, who you want to BE in the world.

I've chosen to format the chapters in a slightly unusual way. Each chapter/mantra opens with the mantra itself. Twice. That's intentional. In order for these mantras to become powerfully useful for you faster, we need to get you to repeat them multiple times in your mind. We can call this "getting in the reps." We're getting in repetitions of reciting the mantras. We are burning them into your neural network so that you can access them more effortlessly sooner.

Throughout each chapter, if the mantra is articulated, it's in bold print. I encourage you to read the mantra deliberately to yourself—or even out loud—to get in more reps. And, finally, each chapter ends with yet another repetition of the mantra. Please read it slowly and anchor for yourself what the mantra means—and its purpose.

These mantras are some of the most valuable tools that I have been able to access in my craft helping people create their lives on their terms, more effortlessly and rapidly. My desire for you is that they serve you as profoundly as they have served me and the thousands of folks I have shared them with over the years.

.

1

Live Above the O-Line!

Live Above the O-Line! As long as we're awake, we are interpreting reality in one of three ways: low-grade, neutral or high-grade. If today is a Friday, a high-grade interpretation of that could be, "Oh, this is so great! This is the beginning of the weekend. I'm so happy."

But, if your days off are Wednesday and Thursday, your interpretation could be, "Oh man. Back to the grind." That's a low-grade interpretation.

And then the other alternative is neutral, which would be articulated simply as, "Today is Friday."

Another example is, "I am holding a blue pen." That's a neutral interpretation. "Is-ness," I sometimes call it. There's no charge to that. There's no positive charge where I'm excited about that. There's no negative charge where I'm upset about it. It's just is-ness.

That's what the "O-Line" is. The "O" in "The O-Line" refers to the *observation* line. An observation is a neutral interpretation.

Here is a diagram that illustrates all this.

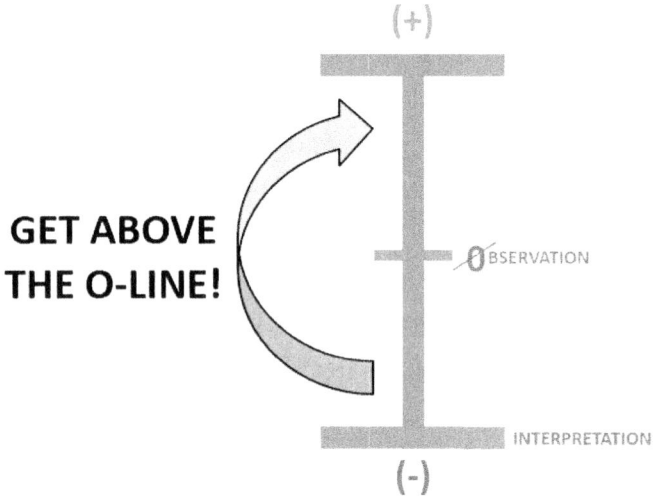

So, again, there are three possibilities for how we interpret reality: high-grade, neutral or low-grade. And the "O" in "The O-Line" refers to an observation, which is a completely neutral interpretation.

You could easily make the argument that the entire purpose of Mental Toughness Training is to systematically, over time and with loads of practice, eliminate your low-grade interpretations so that ultimately—and this is no joke—your lowest grade interpretation of reality would be neutral. Or is-ness.

Let's take another example. You're driving in the middle of the desert in the summertime, and you get a flat tire, and you have no spare (this is a real life example, by the way—more on that in a moment).

A popular and very likely interpretation of this circumstance to the untrained mind would be, "Oh, my God, this totally sucks! I can't believe this is happening to me!" And that is obviously an example of a low-grade interpretation.

With practice, however, what's possible is that your interpretation could be something like, "Hmm. I have a flat. I sure didn't see that coming. What do you know about that?" That's a neutral interpretation of reality. A simple acknowledgement of what is true in the moment, without any emotional charge whatsoever.

Or, with a ton of training, your response could be even better. It could be something like, "Wow! I sure didn't see this coming. I can't wait to see what excellence I create out of this! Because I create from all circumstances! This is the best damn thing that could've

33

happened!"

(That is pretty darn close to how my former coach and dear friend, Steve Hardison, actually responded when he discovered that he was getting a flat tire in the middle of the desert in Arizona in June in 120F heat with no spare. And when I asked him how he is able to have that immediate initial response to something that most people would be outraged over, he answered, "Years and years of practice!")

Let's repeat some of that because it's really what we're working towards here with all of this Mental Toughness Training business. Fundamentally what we are doing this work for is to strengthen our ability to get as fast as possible to creation from all circumstances. Put another way, we're practicing strengthening our ability to respond to all of life with enthusiasm—including the situations that we historically and habitually respond to with unconscious, instantaneous, effortless, low-grade reactions.

"I have a flat tire. I didn't see that coming. I cannot wait to see what excellence I create out of this."

With practice (again, TONS OF IT), that is an available response to the situation. I'm not saying that

that particular response to a flat tire is THE response that anyone should have. I AM saying that it isn't even *available* as a response to the untrained mind. You cannot choose that response without the practice.

The mantra **Live Above the O-Line!** Is a powerful one that reminds us that we have been conditioned to respond to so much of life problematically, or in other words, below The O-Line. When I'm below The O-Line—having a problem with what is—I am deactivating all forms of intelligence, virtually making it impossible for me to be amazing. *Absolutely* making it impossible for me to *feel* amazing.

The mantra, **Live Above the O-Line** is a reminder to catch yourself when you are in a low-grade emotional state that isn't serving you in that moment, and to elevate your thinking in that instant so that your mood elevates immediately. When you do that, everything in you shifts **up**. You feel better, and that activates all the neurotransmitters (like dopamine and serotonin) that act as on-switches for all the intelligence centers of the brain and gut. And that is when we are most likely to be excellent and to create excellence.

And it's all learned. So with the practice of catching

myself when I'm feeling unpleasant and replacing that reaction with a high-grade interpretation, I am practicing systematically reducing the amount of time I spend having a problem with reality. In other words, I'm reducing the amount of time I'm spending below The O-Line—and therefore I'm increasing the amount of time that I'm living above The O-Line, activating all forms of intelligence and making the creation of excellence faster and more effortless.

Live Above the O-Line!

2

The "How?" Is in the "What"

The "How?" Is in the "What." There is a longer, slightly fancier version of this mantra that I learned from one of my favorite teachers, Deepak Chopra:

> *"Inherent within your desires are the mechanics for their own fulfillment."*

I prefer to simplify things, so I simply say, **"The 'How?' Is in the 'What.'"**

Basically, what it boils down to is that we don't need to consume ourselves with HOW our wants and desires are going to unfold, because those details are already embedded within the desires themselves—much like software pre-packaged inside a new computer.

The #1 mistake that I have witnessed people making in the pursuit of their desires is unnecessary waiting. And there are a multitude of reasons that people put unnecessary time in between themselves and realizing their wants. For example, people wait until they have a certain amount of savings in the bank before they feel financially safe. They wait until they have a certain title or degree before they feel competent. They wait until they win a golf tournament before they feel like they belong on the PGA Tour. Or they simply wait for good results before they feel good.

But possibly the most popular reason that people put so much unnecessary time between themselves and their desires is the "How" obstacle.

Let me explain this with a short story.

Many years ago, I was at my sister's house watching a football game on TV. At the time, she only had one child, Benny, and he was an infant. He came crawling into the family room from the kitchen and my sister yelled to me, "Hey, Benny is coming your way! Can you keep an eye on him?" I said, "Of course."

Earlier, I had tossed my car keys up onto the mantle above the fireplace and I was thinking nothing of it. As soon as Benny came crawling into the family room where I was watching the game, he started crawling in my direction. Naturally, I thought he was crawling to come see Uncle Chris.

I was wrong. He blew right past me and kept crawling closer to the brick fireplace, all the while getting more and more of my attention.

Now, let's back it up a touch. As soon as Benny came into the family room, he must have seen my car keys glistening up on the shelf; they lay beneath a canned light. I wasn't aware of this at the time, but he wasn't crawling toward Uncle Chris—he was crawling toward the shiny object in the sky.

Let's pause to acknowledge something critical to the story and to the meaning of the mantra, "The How is in the What." When Benny came into the room and saw the shiny thing (the keys) up in the air, what happened was magnificent—and what DIDN'T happen was every bit as magnificent.

Let's start with what DIDN'T happen.

What Benny DIDN'T do was wait. There was no waiting. No pausing. No consideration of "how." He did NOT think to himself anything like, "Man, I'd sure love to check out that shiny thing up there in the sky, but HOW in the heck would I ever pull that off?! I mean, it's five feet up in the air, and I'm only two feet tall and can barely even stand up! HOW in the world…?"

He didn't stop to reflect upon HOW. He hadn't learned to hesitate. He hadn't learned yet that you "need" to have clarity on how things are going to work out before you take action and move towards your desires (see the chapter on the mantra "Move Towards").

He saw something intriguing. It became an object of desire. And in the very next moment, he started crawling towards it without any curiosity whatsoever about the "how."

Now back to the story. Benny passed me by and reached the fireplace. He had my undivided attention because I wanted to make sure he didn't hit his mouth or his head on the bricks. He was looking up, making baby noises. I was perplexed by his behavior until I followed his gaze to the top of the mantle, saw the keys, and realized that THAT was what he was curious about.

I got off my butt, grabbed the keys, and placed them on the floor in front of him.

POOF! He got what he wanted. And all he did was crawl in the direction of the "what" and then make a little noise. Uncle Chris did all the damn work!

He manifested his desire with virtually effortless ease.

Isn't that great?

You see, in this case, *I* was the "mechanics," or the "how." Benny activated the "how" by moving towards his "what" and making some noise. He didn't need to concern himself with how, or even IF he'd get what he wanted. He moved toward his desire and let the mechanics (Uncle Chris) do the work for him.

It doesn't always work out so obviously effortlessly as it did with Benny and the keys, perhaps. But who cares? We don't need to wait to see how our desires will unfold before taking immediate and bold action.

We don't need to paralyze ourselves into inaction with the "HOW?!" curiosity. Why? Because…

The "How?" is in the "What."

3

I Use History but Don't Permit History to Use Me

I Use History but Don't Permit History to Use Me. There's a story about arguably the greatest golfer in history, Jack Nicklaus. One day, while giving a public clinic to some amateur golfers, Jack was telling a story and mentioned offhand that he had never three-putted the final hole of a major tournament. He continued on with his story when a member in the audience raised his hand and said,

"Pardon me, Mr. Nicklaus, I don't mean to interrupt, but—and with all due respect—you actually three-putted on 18 at last year's Masters tournament."

Jack gave his iconic smirk and replied, "I'm sorry, Sir. You are incorrect." And then he started back in with his story.

Once again the gentlemen apologetically interrupted and said, "Again, I mean no disrespect at all, Mr.

Nicklaus, but I have it recorded. I just watched it. You three-putted the 18th at Augusta last year."

Again, the famous smirk followed by, "No disrespect at all, sir, but you're mistaken."

And on he went with the story. Just as the attendee was about to assert his claim for the third time, his friend beside him grabbed him and said, "Put your damn hand down, fool. Don't you see what he's telling you?! He's deleted that from his memory banks."

(There are hundreds of these stories about Jack's "inability" to recollect his losses. I may not have gotten the details perfect here, but the point is fully intact.)

This story is a perfect example of one of the most powerful Mental Toughness Tools in the toolbox. It's called Selective Memory. It can be abused to avoid responsibility (you must have your own stories about your kids and spouses!), but it can also be used brilliantly to accelerate the creation of mastery.

It's paradoxical. And it works. Here's how.

Jack Nicklaus deleted the memory of the three-putt (no golfer likes to three-jiggle) on the 18th hole of a major. He erased it like I just did the last sentence that I wrote here because I didn't like it. I'm the author here, so I get to do that. Jack is the author of his life story so he has the AUTHORity to delete—or HIGHLIGHT—whatever he pleases.

We all have that authority. The authority to script our stories in the ways that best serve us. Is it delusion? Hell, yeah! Is it lying? Nope. It ain't a lie if you believe it, is it? And who cares anyway? It isn't malicious. In fact, it's powerful. The friend of the guy who kept insisting on being historically accurate learned from Jack in that moment. Jack's self-delusion served that guy, and likely everyone else in the crowd. He was modeling power.

And for those of you who are struggling right now with the okayness of denial, here's the great paradox in all of this. After Jack three-putted that 18th hole of a major tournament, he practiced putting for weeks on end like a madman. If anyone asked him why he was spending all day on the putting greens practicing, you know what he DIDN'T say?

Yeah, you know.

He didn't say, "Because I three-putted eighteen at The Masters, damnit!"

What DID he say? "Because this is what the best putter in history does."

Here's the biggest distinction in this mantra/lesson. You can extract the lesson from the event AND delete the event. Get the growth out of the experience AND delete it once you have. You may not always want to delete the experience. It's your call. You can. But if you do, get the learning first. YOU HAVE TO GET THE LEARNING FIRST!

So, using history means slowing down enough after the undesired event/outcome to truly explore what the learning or growth opportunity is. And take as long as is needed to get that done.

And not permitting history to use you means exercising your authority to do whatever you damn well please with that story—which includes the options of rewriting it or even deleting it entirely from the memory banks.

I Use History but Don't Permit History to Use Me.

4

I Choose Peace Amidst Chaos

I Choose Peace Amidst Chaos. This one has served me quite well over time. I learned it from one of my favorite teachers, the late, great Dr. Wayne Dyer. I had this very mantra written on a sticky note on my dashboard for about two years while I was experiencing some stuff that most would consider quite adverse.

This reMINDer helps us remember that all of our emotional states are choices. We choose our states with our thinking. We have access to every state in every moment of every day of our lives. Isn't that amazing?

It is—IF we can remember AND exercise that choice.

Thus, the word "choose" is the operative word in this mantra. I CHOOSE peace. You could replace the word peace with any other state and it's equally powerful. I choose enthusiasm, for example. I choose compassion. I choose gratitude. You could even replace peace with the

46

word frustration; it might not be the smartest choice, but at least it IS a choice.

But I particularly love the exact phrasing of the mantra the way it is. **I Choose Peace Amidst Chaos.** Isn't it amazing that the option of peace even *exists* amidst chaos?

Wayne Dyer used to tell a funny story about how he came up with this mantra. He had eight children. Yeah, eight! He'd load them all into his Chevy Suburban to drive them to school. Can you imagine all the chaos that ensued inside that vehicle?!

So he used the sticky note option as well. He wrote this mantra on a sticky note and placed it right in front of his face on the dashboard, so that when the kids went nuts, he reMINDed himself that he didn't have to join the chaos.

How powerful is that? He not only didn't need to join the chaos, but he could also choose to be the calm in the storm.

It's very liberating to remember that you have that option available to you at all times. And it's even more liberating to choose it. Think of some of the more chaotic situations that regularly occur in your life.

You have back-to-back-to-back-to-back Zoom meetings. You're getting fried. (I actually have a MUCH better solution suggestion for this circumstance than a mantra—don't schedule yourself like that. But until you are able to revise your scheduling agreements, this mantra can really help.) Have this mantra on a sticky note on the side of your computer monitor. Look at it. And follow its instructions to CHOOSE peace in that moment.

Practicing choosing peace amidst chaos in the smaller chaotic life circumstances, like kids arguing and back-to-back meetings and traffic, will develop your "peace choosing muscle" so that when you find yourself in a much more threatening or significant chaotic situation (like former Tough Talks Podcast guests, SWAT Commander Jeff Nyce in a hostage crisis, or USMC Major Alan Zygowicz rescuing soldiers in combat via helicopter in Viet Nam, or Rtd. Green Beret Dr. Joseph Long in the midst of Guerilla Warfare) you'll have the ability to exercise that same choice to experience peace internally so that you can rapidly problem-solve. Like a blackbelt in Emotional Mastery. Naturally most of us will never find ourselves in THAT level of chaos—I HOPE! But with the repetitions of choosing peace amidst normal daily chaos, when a more significant event goes chaotic in your day—like a sales pitch gone haywire—you got this.

I Choose Peace Amidst Chaos.

5

There's No Such Thing as "Failure"— There Are Only Results

There's No Such Thing as "Failure"—There Are Only Results. If you had to explain to someone who'd never learned what the term "failure" meant, what would you tell them?

Can you recall when you first learned what the term meant? I can't, so I must have been very young when I learned it.

So just now I Googled it. The first definition I saw was "lack of success." So then I Googled "success." It said, "The accomplishment of an aim or purpose."

If those were the ways we all thought of success and failure, I could live with that. Failure, then, is simply the lack of accomplishing an aim or purpose. No part of that implies that any of that sucks. So where did the negative connotation of failure come from? When did failure get such a crappy reputation?

Now, for simplicity's sake, let's say there are only two types of outcomes:

1. You get what you want.
2. You don't.

To the Mentally Tough mind both of those outcomes are equally valuable in distinct ways.

When we get what we want the value is obvious. We get to celebrate that.

When we don't get what we want, this is equally valuable in its own unique way because that's when we get to grow. As humans we are designed for growth! Yet, we've been conditioned to believe that it's a real problem when we don't get what we want.

The mantra **There's No Such Thing as "Failure"— There Are Only Results**, like all our mantras, is an enthusiastic one. When we realize that all results have equal and uniquely distinct value, we know that we can't lose.

And given the fact that we're designed for growth, thank God for when we don't get what we want— because now we have an opportunity to grow.

There's No Such Thing as "Failure"—There Are Only Results.

6

Ain't Bad, Just Is

Ain't Bad, Just Is. William Shakespeare wrote a line in Hamlet that said, "There is nothing either good or bad, but thinking makes it so." The only place in the universe where a problem occurs is in the neocortex of a human being, which is the only place where judgment can occur.

So nothing—and I mean *nothing*, including all the things that we think of as purely tragic—is actually "bad." It just is.

An event is.

No good, no bad. Just is.

Until we use our ability to judge and label it. This sounds ridiculously insensitive to many people. It isn't. "Insensitive" is also a judgment. An interpretation. Whatever I might say isn't sensitive or insensitive. It isn't good or bad. It just IS. Until you label it something.

There's a saying: "Like water off a duck's back." The saying isn't "Like water off a human's back," because we don't roll like that. We aren't like ducks, whose

52

feathers are designed so that water literally slides right off them (have you ever seen a soggy duck?). We don't let stuff go quickly. And the reason we don't is because we've been conditioned to judge, and to *hold* that judgment. We've been conditioned to argue in support of our judgment. We go to war against each other because of our allegiance to our judgment.

But our judgments are never correct or incorrect. They're simply judgments. Or interpretations.

Now, if we're interested in creating massive amounts of excellence in our lives at the fastest rate possible, we really do want to practice stopping having a problem with reality. We want to pay very close attention to our judgments and ask ourselves, "Does this interpretation serve me and others right now?" Or is it getting in the way?

When we have a problem with reality, when we're complaining, when we think something is really bad, we're deactivating all forms of creative genius. In other words, we're paralyzing ourselves. We're immobilizing our ability to create and grow.

We're simply spending time having a problem with what is, and simultaneously causing dis-ease. We're definitely causing emotional dis-ease, and also quite possibly creating physiological disease.

Ain't Bad, Just Is, is one of the first go-to mantras that I use in the milliseconds after I catch myself complaining.

It's the ultimate neutralizer mantra. It's like an antacid for emotional heartburn.

So, for example, say I have a huge business deal that is potentially very lucrative. It looks really good, and then for whatever reason, it abruptly disappears. Most likely my initial reaction would be something along the lines of, "This plain sucks. This is horrible! Damn it! I can't believe this happened."

That's all learned response. Learned and rehearsed. We practice that response every day when we don't get what we want. So we are very good at that response. (We get very good at whatever we practice a lot.)

Imagine instead that your auto-response to the big business deal falling through is, "Oh, how fascinating. I didn't see that coming."

That's neutral. Visualize that. It's a possibility. And it will get you to creativity much faster. You're not wasting time arguing with reality, with what just happened. So you can put your energy into what you want to create.

I use **Ain't Bad, Just Is** sort of like a gateway mantra. Like I say, it's the ultimate neutralizer mantra when something seems like it's gone south. So I often follow it up with "Well, not only is it not 'bad'—it actually could be AMAZING!"

(And there's a mantra for that, too—what are the odds? That mantra is, "Every set of circumstances can be created from, if viewed masterfully." But we'll get to that one later on in the book.)

So **Ain't Bad, Just Is** is a perfectly effective complaint neutralizer—and it's actually true.

Ain't Bad, Just Is.

7

ALL IN!

ALL IN! In addition to being a nice, concise mantra, **ALL IN!** is actually a state of mind. It's the psychological state we're in when we're infinitely committed to something—to anything: a goal or a mission, a desire to be some way, to have something, to get something, to do something, to accomplish something. It's a state of mind, and we can choose it like any other state. And it just so happens to be THE most powerful state available to us for getting things done! And getting them done well and fast!

We have access to every single human emotional state that exists. Therefore, we have access to the **ALL IN!** state in every moment of our lives, without anything in the world being different. **ALL IN!** is just one of the many states we have available to us.

I could choose to think my way into misery right now. I could choose to think my way into serenity right now. I could choose to think my way into competence right now. I can choose to think my way into panic. I can also choose to think my way into the **ALL IN!** or infinitely committed state. The uniqueness of that particular state of mind is that when I'm **ALL IN!**—or infinitely committed—the possibility of failure is non-existent in my field of consciousness.

In my mind, when I'm **ALL IN!** the possibility of not having, being, doing or getting what I want is not on my radar. I'm too busy doing what it takes—taking immediate, bold, and masterful action—to entertain the possibility of failure.

The irony here is that we're actually **ALL IN!** almost all the time, but *with small things that don't matter to us*. Buttoning a shirt, writing words, taking a sip of coffee, even driving a car, which is one of the most dangerous things that we can do from day to day. I'm going to the store to pick up some groceries. There's no part of me that entertains the possibility of not being able to succeed in this bad-ass grocery store mission! I don't doubt my ability to get to the store, when in fact, there are so many reasons why I actually might not get there. There are many possibilities that could prevent me from succeeding in my mission to get the groceries, but I'm not entertaining any of them. I'm **ALL IN!**

So there's irony here (there's irony everywhere). When we're pursuing things that *really* matter to us, THAT'S when we bring doubt into the equation. Isn't that funny? Whenever we are in the midst of the creation of some miracle for ourselves, some wonderful vision, some task, some goal, some great desire—that's when we bring doubt into the experience. And as a consequence, we decrease the probability of success.

Upgrade the important experiences in your life from "goals" to DECISIONS! The difference between a goal and a decision is monumental: a goal leaves the door open for the possibility of failure, whereas a decision does not. The decision-making state is synonymous with the **ALL IN!** state. So when you're pursuing something really valuable or important to yourself, make sure that you're **ALL IN!**

ALL IN!

8

The Outer World Is a Reflection of the Inner World

The Outer World Is a Reflection of the Inner World. In other words, what I have going on in my life (outer world), is the direct result of what I've got going on in my mind (inner world).

This means I have a lot of incentive to strengthen my inner world! If I care about how my life is going, then I must also care about strengthening the quality of my inner world experience.

If I have chaos in my life, I have chaos in my mind. People who are owners and creators of their lives love that fact, because it means they can create their lives by changing their inner world experience. People who choose to live as victims of circumstance can't even hear that.

It bears repeating. What I have going on in my life is the direct result of what I've got going on in my mind.

Now, if I have abundance in my life it is because I have abundance in my mind. If I have both chaos and abundance in my life, it's because I have both chaos and abundance in my mind, which is probably the case for most of us.

I will never be able to sustainably and powerfully redesign my life in a way that suits me, that I love, if I cannot strengthen the inner world. Most of us have never been taught how to really fortify the quality of our thinking or the quality of the inner world. We haven't been taught how to master our moods. We didn't have classes on any of that in grade school or high school or college or anywhere.

One of the keys to being able to create our lives on our terms is taking complete ownership of the fact that what I have in my life is the result of what I have going on in my mind. If I think life sucks, I'm probably experiencing it that way. If I think I'm going to lose, I increase my odds of losing. And the opposite is true: if I think I'm going to succeed, I increase my odds—and even if I don't, I will tend to find what's good in an apparent failure. Just knowing this gets me looking at my life in a whole new way. And then I can get busy doing the work of upgrading the way I'm choosing to interpret reality. Only then will I be able to most effortlessly create my life on my terms.

The Outer World Is a Reflection of the Inner World.

9

Every Set of Circumstances Can Be Created From—IF Viewed Masterfully

***Every* Set of Circumstances Can Be Created from— IF Viewed Masterfully.** (Emphasis on the words *every* and *IF.)*

Put another way, we all possess the ability to create some magic, some excellence, something fantastic, from every single set of circumstances, without exception. But it's totally contingent upon our willingness and ability to interpret those circumstances from a place of mental mastery.

When I'm in complaint, it is impossible—literally impossible—for me to create anything excellent.

When I'm in complaint, fundamentally what that means is that I'm struggling against what is, fighting against reality. I can do that, of course, and I'll only lose one hundred percent of the time.

So, if I can practice *responding* to what happens

instead of struggling against it—particularly in circumstances when I don't get what I want or something occurs that I wasn't hoping or planning for, expecting or wanting—if I can practice responding to that with grace (at worst with patience, at best with enthusiasm), then I can do the real magic, which is to get to creation as fast as possible.

So: event → action.

Event → immediate action.

Undesirable event? Get into immediate action. Get into the inquiry, "I wonder what I can create from this undesired outcome?"

Let's take an example. I come out of the mall and my car is stolen. The normal response would be, "Oh crap, this really sucks." And I can make the argument that that's actually the normal response because that's a *learned* response. We grow up thinking that if someone takes something that's ours from us, it's a bad thing.

But what if the normal response is instead, "Oh, how fascinating!"

In fact, I don't actually care what the "normal" response is; what matters is what we can *do*, which is to respond with something like, "Wow, I didn't see that coming! Not what I asked for! Alright. I wonder what amazing thing I will create from this, so that in a year from now, I'll have one hell of a great story!" Then I'd be able to say I was glad my car was stolen, particularly because of the way I responded to it. And who knows what it'll be that I'll create from the event? We don't need to know. That's the beauty of it.

When I get into creation—especially with enthusiasm—as fast as possible after any event, that's when the magic happens. And it takes practice, but it leads us to see that ***Every* Set of Circumstances Can Be Created From—IF Viewed Masterfully.**

***Every* Set of Circumstances Can Be Created From— IF Viewed Masterfully.**

10

Start with Perfect

Start with Perfect. When I ask my new coaching clients what they would love to create for themselves, I NEVER trust their first responses. It's not that I think they're lying to me. It's that I think they're lying to *themselves*.

Over time, we have all been conditioned to believe that what we REALLY want is either going to be very difficult or "hard," maybe even TOO challenging to create. It's at best improbable but maybe even impossible, completely unattainable.

And then we settle. As a consequence of being thoroughly convinced that our greatest desires are not imminently available to us, we stop even entertaining those desires and settle for what we believe is more "practical" or "realistic"—and that's tragic.

One time I met with a prospective coaching client who was a high school swimmer. We never ended up actually working together (but that's irrelevant; what happened in our exploratory session is what's perfectly relevant here). As I do with all prospective clients, I asked him what it was that he wanted to create for himself. Here's how that conversation went:

Me: So, if we work together, what's the big outcome that you would want to create for yourself?

Him: I want to make States.

Me: Okay. So, you want to qualify to compete in the state championship tournament?

Him: Yes.

Me: If you qualify, do you care how you do in States?

Him: Well, I mean, I wouldn't mind doing well.

Me. Okay. So, we would train you so that you could "do well" at States?

Him: Sure.

Me: How well?

Him: (pause)

Me: (silently witnessing him starting to get more honest with himself)

Him: Well, it would be cool to place.

Me: Which place?

Him: Well, I guess First Place would be great.

Me: To be clear, Buddy, I am not trying to influence

you to want anything bigger than what you really want. I actually don't care what you want. What I care deeply about is that you GET what you want, so we need to get clear on what it is.

Him: I understand.

Me: So, what is it that you really want?

Him: I want to win states and then swim for Stanford.

Me: Oh. Okay. That's a solid swim program they've got there. Would you want to go on scholarship, or does that not matter to you?

Him: Of course I would!

Me: How about this. You go do some thinking and get really clear on what it actually is that you truly want for yourself. When you're clear, let's reconnect.

This happens all the time. Unless I'm talking to a five-year-old. Five-year-olds have yet to be well-educated about their "limitations," so they have perfect clarity and absolutely zero self-consciousness in telling it to people. "I want to be a fisherman and an astronaut and the President and a fireman, and I want to live in a castle on a cloud with a waterslide for when I want to come down to see my friends."

How pure is that?! In that child's unadulterated mind,

there is enthusiastic clarity on desires. That child hasn't been told that what they want is "unrealistic"—or worse, "impossible"—so their desires are fully intact. But give it a few years and they'll learn. They'll start learning to shrink the think. And each of us has had that same education.

The mantra **Start with Perfect** is a reMINDer to unlearn the limitations and to permit yourself to start your thinking with what perfect looks like. We can't create what we want if we don't know what we want.

What do you REALLY want?

Start with Perfect.

11

Nervous Can't Exist in Service

Nervous Can't Exist in Service. Several years ago, I was backstage at a massive conference in Chicago about to deliver the closing keynote for a week-long global sales kickoff for a large international software company. It was the biggest event I'd ever spoken at. By far.

There were thousands of people in the audience and thousands more tuning in from around the world. There was a huge, forty-two-foot main screen and two twenty-four footers on the right and left. It was quite the theatrical event. Before I went onstage for my closing keynote, I was sitting backstage in this massive production "village." It was a city of wires and cables and people wearing black staring at screens. And there were some technical challenges.

So there I was, sitting alone, ready to go. I had my game face on, as I always do before any big performance. But then there were these technical challenges. There was a twenty-minute delay, and I could peek out through an opening in the screens where I could see the audience. People were getting confused and a little impatient. I heard a guy near me backstage raising his voice. I looked over and saw him getting really angry. He was one of the people who'd hired me; he was typically a very smooth sailor, but he was having words with the Production Manager, and the whole vibe of the event—in that moment—started to feel pretty bad.

And I, in turn, started to get pretty nervous. Actually close to panicked.

I lost my game face completely.

I remember thinking to myself, "How ironic is this? I'm a Mental Toughness Coach about to go give a closing keynote on the power of Mental Toughness, and I'm sitting backstage losing my shit!"

I thought to myself, "Well, we can't have this happen. I need to get out of this state." And I broke it down. I actually got curious. After all, I had time! And I thought to myself, "Why is this happening? Why would I ever get nervous? Where does this nervousness come from?" And I realized, pretty quickly, that it was completely egocentric. I was only nervous because I was being an arrogant jerk, thinking somehow that this moment was about me.

I was getting worried because I was concerned about whether or not I was going to do okay. Which is very childish, very sophomoric, because it was very disconnected from the whole point of the event and my presence at it—which was to serve. I was a servant. I was there to deliver some goods, some messages, some practices, some disciplines that would help people's lives, that would help them reduce the unnecessary settling, struggling, and suffering in their lives.

I mean, what a gift this was for me to be able to do this. What a privilege!

But I wasn't excited to bring my own gift because I forgot that I was the gift-giver. And I got into my ego and thought I was some kind of performance artist and that I needed to do a good job. And if I didn't do a good job, bad things would happen . . . and all other sorts of nonsense. So I came up with the mantra **Nervous Can't Exist in Service.**

When I remembered that my whole mission there was simply to give gifts, like someone going to a birthday party with a beautiful gift that you're proud to give away, the nervousness *instantaneously* dissolved. It wasn't about me. It was about the service, the gift.

So now whenever I'm about to do anything, any kind of performance, any kind of event before which I've noticed that I'm starting to get nervous—I remember this means I'm acting out of ego right there, and I use this mantra to squash it, to instantly get right back into peace and servitude. And the mantra, of course, is **Nervous Can't Exist in Service.**

Nervous Can't Exist in Service.

12

Everything is Unfolding Exactly as it Should

Everything Is Unfolding Exactly as it Should. That is not a "looking at life through rose-colored-glasses" mantra. (In fact, none of these mantras are.) This is actually based on scientific facts. This mantra, **Everything Is Unfolding Exactly as it Should**—and the longer version continues with "and nothing needs to be anything other than exactly what it is"—actually came from my study of astrophysics.

When I was floundering exploring careers after college, one of the vocations I was considering was astrophysics, because I've always been fascinated with the big questions like: Where does this all come from? Where's it all going?? How does it even work???

Maybe the most powerful lesson I took away from that year of study is that *for fifteen billion years, this*

73

universe has been unfolding with flawless choreography.

There are millions of factors (maybe billions, maybe trillions) that needed to be precisely as they were in order for *any* of this—life, universe, cosmos—to occur.

For example, milliseconds after the big bang, the ratio of particles to anti-particles needed to be precisely what it was—p r e c i s e l y what it was, that exact ratio— *in order for anything to occur.*

If the ratio had been slightly off from what it was in favor of either particles or anti-particles, then it would have been a big bang immediately followed by a big crunch. Nothing would have happened. Imagine a big bang, and then a puff of smoke that quickly dissipates. That's what it would've been like. There'd be nothing.

But, instead, it was perfect.

Everything has been perfect. The ratio of helium to hydrogen in stars has to be exactly what it is in order for stars to go supernova—that's when they go Kaboom. Our star, our sun, is at its midlife—4.5 billion years old—and in 4.5 more billion years, it's gonna blow up!

And when that happens, where we're sitting, where you're sitting right now, that'll be FIRE. As far as we know, a supernova is the most cataclysmic event that can occur in the universe. Yet that most violent event generates the heavy elements of carbon and oxygen—the building blocks of life. In other words, a supernova is the birthplace of what the universe needs to create life.

So without that there'd be nothing.

All of life itself could only ever occur from these perfect ratios.

The mass of our moon and the distance that it is from our planet Earth, has to be precisely what it is in order to create an atmosphere that's amenable to life. That list of factors, variables that need to be precisely what they are for any of this to occur, is *endless*.

If I can remember that, I can stay in a state of awe, gratitude, enthusiasm, and creativity. This mantra is very helpful for that, particularly when stuff doesn't go the way I think it should. That's when ego takes over—if I let it—and I start to experience life as a problem. The only place in this cosmos where a "problem" exists is in the neocortex of a human being.

That's where judgment occurs. That's where we forget that everything is unfolding exactly as it should.

So this mantra is very useful as a reminder that when things aren't going as I think they should, it's okay, because the universe has our back. It had it even before we got here.

Everything Is Unfolding Exactly as it Should.

13

Vibe Up!

Vibe Up! One of my great mentors in life, who is also a great friend (actually a soul sister), Dr. Alison Arnold, or "Doc Ali," taught me the following. This is actually the longer version of the mantra **Vibe Up!**

> *We are always either purifying or polluting the environment with our vibes.*

You could re-articulate that to say, "We're always either purifying or polluting the environment with our thoughts."

And the reason that those two sentences are identical is because thoughts are measurable vibrationally.

There's actually a device called a magnetoencephalograph, which looks like a big old-school hair dryer that you pull over your head from above, like in an old hair salon. What it does is literally measure the frequency of the vibration of the content of your mind.

In other words, it's measuring the frequency of your thoughts. It's measuring the vibes. We are constantly emitting vibrations. And those vibrations are very detectable.

We've all heard the phrase, "I get a bad vibe from that guy." People may think that they're using that phrase metaphorically but they aren't. They're actually being literal, because they're detecting a real vibration.

Dogs are great at it. Horses. Swordfish. So many creatures are dialed in on the vibes. They are excellent at sensing and responding to vibes.

Vibe Up! I use this mantra as a reminder to myself to choose to elevate my state all throughout the day, particularly if I'm going into some event that matters to me, even if it's a social gathering.

Before I go into a birthday party with friends and family, I'll actually take a moment and literally elevate my state by choosing to think my way into enthusiasm, joy, celebration, comradery, compassion, and gratitude.

Then I'll walk into the party with this silent, invisible gift that I'm bringing, which is actually detectable. (And it's free! Ha!)

Without having to say a word about it, I am automatically inviting everyone around me to elevate their own states. It's very contagious. Joy and enthusiasm. These high-grade states are very, very contagious.

People, without even knowing it, are accepting those invitations to join you in elevated states. The whole party gets even better. And I'm not just talking about that birthday party. I'm talking about the party of life.

If I'm making a call to customer service, I definitely take a few moments before dialing the number to elevate my vibe. It's a very strategic move. Isn't that great? It increases the probability of good outcomes, AND the participants are almost always happier. Your high vibe influences others to want to participate with you and serve you. Your high vibe drastically increases the odds of a great outcome.

Think of some times or events in your life where it could benefit you (and others) to intentionally **Vibe Up!** beforehand. And get into the practice of doing that.

Vibe Up!

14

I Am Infinite Possibilities

The mantra is **I Am Infinite Possibilities.**

Notice that it doesn't say I am *capable* of infinite possibilities.

It says **I *Am* Infinite Possibilities** and that's a much bigger statement.

Everything in the universe, when reduced down to its most common, fundamental form, is simply vibrating energy fields localized into different physical forms. Like you, me, a trashcan, a car, a flagpole, a planet—fundamentally everything is a quark—a particle you can't break down any further into other particles. Quantum physics illustrates that.

Therefore, I am instantly and inextricably connected to everything that exists across space-time. That's actually a mantra of its own, and it's also part of the explanation of this mantra, and I'm going to repeat it. *I am instantly and inextricably connected to all that exists across space- time.* (There's a lot of cool research on the instantaneous accessibility of information that we won't get into here, but it's intricately related to our connection to everything.)

As an inextricably and instantly connected, localized form of some of the energy of the universe, I'm not "capable" of infinite possibilities. I AM all those possibilities.

So what do I want to do with this mantra? I want to remember that whenever I have the arising of a "Yeah, but . . ." immediately after getting a great idea, a grand mission or desire—I want to squash that! Because that "Yeah, but . . ." is saying maybe I can have a brilliant idea, BUT it's probably not *possible* to bring it to fruition. So I stop before I start.

So I'm going to squash that "Yeah, but" and think, "To hell with 'maybe'! To hell with, 'I wonder if I can...' To hell with, 'I don't know how I would ever. I don't know how that would work. I don't know if I can. I don't know if that's realistic. I don't know if that's possible.'"

SQUASH ALL THAT like you would with a hammer, with the mantra:

I Am Infinite Possibilities.

15

I ~~have~~ GET TO!

I ~~have~~ GET TO! One of the first thoughts people often wake up with in the morning is, "Aw, man, what do I have to do today?"

And it's not a light-hearted thought. It's more of an obligatory, I'd-rather-not kind of thought. It's not very powerful—in fact, it's a weak thought, and it's a complete passion- and creative-genius-killer. It's also *learned.* Which is great news. Because it can be *un*learned!

My late mentor and dearest of friends, Jim Myers, taught me this mantra/practice. He was one of the happiest and most successful and most loved and respected people I have ever met. (No coincidence that those are all inextricably linked.) He ran an Executive Forum, and he would open each meeting with some Zen Master-like koan or story or teaching. One of his favorite messages to RE-mind his clients was to choose to live in a "GET TO" versus a "have to" world. He very unapologetically advised everyone to replace their "I have to" thoughts with "get to" ones. And to MEAN IT!

And that's the catch: to have the "GET TO" be real.

Waking up and asking yourself, "What do I GET TO do today?" is not some fluffy euphemism or kumbaya crap. It's a discipline that, with time, evolves into a brilliant, light, joy-filled way of experiencing life fully and intelligently and masterfully.

Jim's advice was not just to change the *language* but rather to use the "GET TO" language to change the *attitude*! (That's the magic of mantras!) And that alone changed a lot of lives. Jim changed a lot of lives in a lot of ways, but this one shift, which seems small, is actually monumental. Because the shift from experiencing life problematically to experiencing life enthusiastically is possibly the greatest unlearning shift that exists!

What is central to having your "What do I GET TO do today?" question and answer be sincere is your willingness to own all of your life. Victims of circumstance will never understand this because they are living in a "happening TO me" world. Victims of circumstances have weak, untrained minds. Those types of minds make the owners of those minds entirely vulnerable to all the outer world. When you choose to be the opposite of a victim—that is, a Creator—you take ownership of the fact that whatever you have going on in your life is a co-creation of yours.

So, when you awaken each day, whatever is on the agenda is your creation. For example, your job and everything that comes with it—you choose it. You created it and you choose it every day. If it sucks so bad, change your choice and don't let limiting, learned beliefs have you doubt your resourcefulness and your ability to create your life on your terms.

I GET TO change my entire life if that pleases me.

When I choose to live in the "GET TO" mentality, possibilities open up for me because I am activating all intelligence centers of the brain with my enthusiasm. I see solutions I wouldn't otherwise see in the "have to" stink. I have brilliant ideas that are impossible to generate in the "have to" mindset. I take a quality of action that is more immediate, bold and masterful than the shoulders-slumped, feet-dragging, woe-is-me victim

I have GET TO!

mindset of "have to" thinking.

Mathematically speaking, you are an incomprehensible improbability (we cover that at least once or twice in other chapters). You won the ultimate lottery—getting into life. You won. We won. WE WON!!! Can you feel that?! EVERYTHING is a **GET TO**—if you'll have it be.

Have it be.

I have GET TO!

16

I Embrace Uncertainty, Paradox and Ambiguity

I Embrace Uncertainty, Paradox and Ambiguity. What could ever be wrong with those three things? Uncertainty, paradox and ambiguity. Yet the conditioning of our past would have us believe that these are actually problems.

Uncertainty—not knowing how things are going to go, how they'll unfold—problem.

Paradox means contradiction—problem.

And ambiguity is a lack of clarity—another problem.

Unless they aren't.

Consider uncertainty. What's interesting is that when I go to a movie for the first time, I'm actually pretty pumped about the fact that I have no idea how it's going to unfold. That actually gives the movie its entertainment value. I actually DON'T want to know what's going to happen, because that ruins it!

What if we treated our lives similarly? What if we embraced the uncertainty and literally practiced loving it.

Same with the seeming—or actual—paradoxes in life. Here's one, for example, in human peak performance: You would think that our greatest ever performances would require enormous amounts of effort, maybe even struggle. That thinking is the birthplace of stupid phrases like "no pain, no gain."

It's so dumb. Don't ever say that.

In fact, if you really study human peak performance, isn't it fascinating that everyone always describes these peak, best-ever performances as *effortless*—or damn close to it? There was never a struggle. That's a paradox. Why would I ever be afraid of *that* paradox?

And where did I learn to have a problem with ambiguity?

We have all been conditioned to believe that we need to have answers to questions like, "How's this going to work? I want to create this. I'm going to start my own business and I want to buy my dream home on a beach somewhere, but how's it going to work? I don't have any clarity whatsoever on how that's possibly going to unfold!"

Personally, I don't want to know. In fact, I probably *can't* know right at the start—and if I let that stop me, I might *never* know, because I won't even start.

The "How?" Is In The What (as you know from an earlier chapter). Let the "How?" present itself. I want to love the ambiguity—and I want to watch the ambiguity fade into amazing clarity as I practice embracing it.

Get ALL IN! and take immediate bold masterful action and Create Miracles.

I Embrace Uncertainty, Paradox and Ambiguity.

17

I Fulfill My Desires With Effortless Ease

I Fulfill My Desires with Effortless Ease. One of the coolest things about being a human is that we are at our best when we feel our best. I have worked with people in the field of peak performance my whole life and isn't it fascinating that every single person who has ever been asked to describe their peak performances—their "Best Evers"—uses descriptors like: *light, fun* and *effortless*?!

That seems to be counter-intuitive, doesn't it? It's in total contradiction to popular phrases like "no pain, no gain." That phrase, by the way, is one of the stupidest phrases in history, because it's completely inconsistent with every shred of human peak-performance research. When people are performing at peak, they're in what is also referred to as "the zone," or the flow state.

Flow is a great word. There's no effort in flow.

So this mantra serves as a powerful reminder that as

humans *we're at our best when we feel our best*, and it really serves us to let the creation of excellence be effortless.

Another paradox is this: I want to work really, really hard at strengthening my mind so that the creation of excellence becomes really, really easy.

I want to use this mantra regularly. I want this one to be part of my daily reprogramming. It's a good one to add to your morning routine.

I Fulfill My Desires with Effortless Ease.

18

Move Towards

Move Towards. This is an amazingly powerful mantra. It's also a kissing cousin of The "How?" Is in the What.

There's a longer, alternative version of it, which is: "Inherent within your desires are the mechanics for their own fulfillment."

So what does this mean for us? It means we want to activate those mechanics as soon as possible. How? By moving towards. **Move towards** your greatest desires. NOW! Stop waiting.

The number one mistake that I have observed humans making in the pursuit of their desires is unnecessary waiting. Putting unnecessary time between ourselves and our greatest desires. The number one reason I've observed us all waiting is what I call *The How Obstacle.*

We've been conditioned to believe that we need to have clarity on *how* something's going to unfold before we commit to it fully and get active pursuing and creating it.

That's nonsense.

In fact, it's fun to *not* know the how, and to activate the *how* by getting clarity on what it is that you *want*—and then **Move Towards** with immediate action.

Activate the mechanics of *how* and **Move Towards.**

Move Towards.

19

Normalize the Miraculous

Normalize The Miraculous.

This mantra is a reminder to make it "normal" to experience life miraculously.

This is a fun mantra, because it's actually a verb. It's like a command: **Normalize the Miraculous!** And what it means is this: we can experience all of life as miraculous, if only we choose to view it that way.

Arguably the greatest scientist in history, Albert Einstein, said, "There are only two ways to view the world. One is as if nothing is a miracle. The other is as if everything is. I choose the latter."

I encourage us all to make that same choice.

Choose to experience all of life as miraculous.

Normalize the Miraculous.

20

My Language Is the Fingerprint of My Thinking

My Language Is the Fingerprint of My Thinking. Another way of saying this is, "Watch your mouth." And I actually think that's more fun. I'm always watching my mouth. I'm watching specifically what comes out of it. And I'm always in the inquiry, "Do I agree with those words I just spoke?"

My language really is a dead giveaway as to what I'm thinking. So if I want to become a thought warrior and ultimately only choose to act upon thoughts that serve me, that maximize the probability of me being who I want to be and creating why I want to create, language is an excellent tool for me to use to examine the quality of my thinking.

So pay attention to what you're saying. I often catch myself in the middle of talking about something and say, "Delete that. I don't even agree with what I just said."

It's a great practice to use your language as a mechanism to profoundly heighten the quality of your thinking.

My Language Is the Fingerprint of My Thinking.

21

I Am Need-less, I Am Worry-free

I Am Need-less, I Am Worry-free. You can make the argument that, no, we really aren't need-less. In order to live we need some things. Only a few. We need air. We need food. We need water. We need shelter. Beyond that we really don't need much, but those are some pretty big needs.

But here's the irony, and this is why I love this mantra so much. When I choose to feel need-less and worry-free is when I make the creation of excellence so much easier.

In fact, I make all of life easier. So to put it a different way, when I choose need-lessness, all of life gets easier.

When I'm feeling needy or when I'm feeling any levels of anxiety, I am compromising all forms of intelligence and therefore I am *minimizing* the probability of creating what I want. So the paradox again is this: the more need-less I am, the more likely I am to create my desire.

Or I could rephrase that into: The less I need my desires, the more likely I am to create them.

I Am Need-less, I Am Worry-free.

22

Create the State, Don't Wait

Create the State, Don't Wait. My entire career has been in the field of helping people upgrade the way they experience life. I help people create their lives on their terms, and do it with less effort.

The most frequently made mistake I have observed people making (myself included!) in the pursuit of their desires and the pursuit of excellence is *waiting*. Unnecessary waiting. Putting unnecessary time between ourselves and what we want and who we want to be. We do that because we've learned to.

For example:

- Waiting to make Club before feeling like an expert sales rep
- Waiting to get a certain GPA in academics before feeling your own genius

- Waiting for acknowledgement to feel competent.
- Athletes—waiting for a win to feel they belong at that level.
- Waiting for "vacation" to feel relaxed (and even then, many don't).

There's an endless list of the ways that we wait. And we've all been conditioned to do that.

Thus the mantra, **Create the State, Don't Wait**. You could follow that up with a question, "Create *what* state?" and the answer is: whatever state is gonna serve you in this moment. And different states will serve you in different moments (just like different mantras).

So, for example, say you're a salesperson and you're about to give a huge presentation on a major account. What emotional states would be handy for you to be in going into that experience?

Well, I'll throw out a few: Competency. Expertise. Confidence. Need-lessness.

Don't wait to see how the presentation starts to go. Don't gauge where you're coming from on how your customer/prospect is responding before you feel those states.

You **Create the State, Don't Wait.**

One of the most magical human superpowers that we have is the ability to create any state—any and every state that exists—in a moment's time, with our thinking. That's fundamental to this mantra. I'll repeat: we have access to every single human emotional state, in every moment of our lives. All we need to do is think our way into it.

So we want to ask ourselves, "What's the state that will serve me now?"

Say my friend's parent just passed away and I'm going to go see that friend. What's an emotional state that would serve me (and my friend) in that instance? Compassion? Empathy? Love? Serenity? Strength? Create them all before you walk into your friend's home.

Create the State, Don't Wait. Don't wait to see how the outer world goes. Don't wait for the outer world to do *anything* before you profoundly manipulate your inner state.

Our emotional states GOVERN how we show up in life. This can be a problem if we don't remember that we can *create the state*.

Our conditioning would have us wait to see how things go. And that's a tragic mistake because it creates an enormous waste of time and a lot of unnecessary human struggle—and worse, suffering.

Before going into any event that you care about, take a few moments to choose to manipulate your thinking. Literally change the content of your thoughts. What kind of thoughts would result in confidence? Competence? Enthusiasm? Certainty? Calmness? Determination? Instead of doubts, *know* you have this. Feel the enthusiasm before you walk through the door. Feel the inner certainty instead of thinking the thoughts that make you doubtful and uncertain. Choose that quality of your thinking so you can think your way into the states that will best serve you. Let it be that simple! Because it can be!

This mantra reminds you that you have the ability to *create the emotional state(s) that will maximize the probability of you being who you want to be, and creating what you want to create—in any circumstance.*

Create the State, Don't Wait.

23

I Relinquish the Need to Defend

I Relinquish the Need to Defend. (This mantra refers specifically to the experience of defending ourselves EMOTIONALLY, not physically.)

We have learned to put enormous amounts of mental energy into defending ourselves when it's not necessary.

We never need to defend ourselves emotionally. Never. In conversation with people, we have learned to take offense to things, and therefore we have practiced going to the effort of defending ourselves when we believe we're being attacked emotionally or psychologically. And even when we are being verbally assaulted, we actually don't need to go to the effort of defending ourselves. Slow that down. Ingest that. Let's make it about YOU. YOU do not need to defend yourself EVER. The only reason you ever do is because you believe that there's a threat present, when in fact, there isn't.

The foundation of the need to defend yourself emotionally or psychologically is born out of the belief that you might not be okay. And that is not true, because the only circumstance in which you wouldn't be okay is when you believe you won't be okay. No one's words could ever offend you. They're just words or opinions. There could even be great truth in the words. There could be great learning opportunities for you in those words. But they're just words. And no words are ever really "offensive"—only our interpretations of them are. The words aren't offensive even if they're meant to be. WE TAKE OFFENSE all by ourselves. (Many people will never get that because they haven't done the work that you are doing—the work that has you reading this book in the first place!)

So imagine this for a moment . . .

You have reprogrammed yourself—your mind—such that you no longer ever go to the effort of defending yourself emotionally, even when someone is clearly attempting to offend you. Instead of taking those words as offensive, you see through the emotion, perfectly peacefully, with curiosity. Maybe even a little excitement for the possibility that there could be something useful for you in those words regardless of how they're being delivered. You are capable of experiencing reality AS IT IS.

And the reality in that moment is simply that someone is speaking words to you. They are expressing some of their thoughts to you. Perhaps in a very aggressive, condescending or even emotionally violent way. Because of your Mental Toughness training, your practice, you are able to remember in that moment that the emotional nature of the communication has actually nothing to do with you.

The content MIGHT. Maybe. Maybe not. But the emotional charge in the other person's delivery has nothing to do with you. It has only to do with their own unhealed hurt. So there's nothing for you to defend.

Because of the practice that you have done, you have the ability to remain in a state of pure peace amidst "chaos" and completely relinquish any effort you might otherwise think you need to expend in defending yourself. Visualize and practice that.

I Relinquish the Need to Defend.

24

You Can't Over-train Your Brain

You Can't Over-train Your Brain. In so many ways, Mental Training is identical to physical training. It takes practice. Much like physical training, if you're going to develop your muscles, you need to do repetitions. Your workouts consist of sets that consist of multiple repetitions. For example, if you want to build your pectoral muscles, you may want to do a bunch of pushups. So you'll do fifteen pushups, and you'll do four sets of them. Those are the reps.

It's the same thing with Mental Training. For example, if you want to strengthen your Emotional Mastery, you'll certainly want to accumulate tens of thousands of repetitions of converting complaints into expressions of gratitude. And by the way, if scientists are correct, we have the opportunity to do that once every eleven seconds. That's how frequently some scientists think that we actually complain. So we could get a rep in every eleven seconds.

Now, unlike physical training, you can't overdo it with Mental Training. You will never get injured. You can't hurt yourself and you will never exhaust yourself with Mental Training. You're elevating the quality of your thinking, which means you're elevating your state, which means not only is it not exhausting, it's actually invigorating.

So unlike physical training, where you really could over-train, and get hurt, in Mental Training, that is an impossibility.

I like to say that the most mentally tough/happiest/ successful people in the world choose to live in a state of *perpetual self-inquiry.* Some people hear that as exhausting, but it isn't.

Perpetually asking oneself questions, like:

How do I feel right now?
What is the state that I'm thinking my way into in this moment?
Is it serving me?
Could it use an upgrade?

If it sounds exhausting when you think about this

practice being perpetual (no days off, no minutes off), you're not getting it. It's not. In fact, it's the opposite of exhausting.

What IS exhausting is living in low-grade states— living below The O-Line. *That* is exhausting.

Here's a paradox for you: every time I go to the effort of elevating my state, of catching myself below The O-Line, if I upgrade my interpretations of reality in that moment, and therefore elevate my state, *I am relieved of the exhaustion.*

You Can't Over-train Your Brain.

25

Do It Anyway, Do It Now

Do It Anyway, Do It Now. This is a great mantra for procrastination elimination. I actually stole this mantra from a young client of mine several years ago. He learned it from his grandfather. It's a mantra about not putting things off. And not putting things off—or, putting it another way: taking immediate action and getting things done rapidly—is a characteristic of people who choose to live powerfully.

So here's the practice. Say for example that I'm in my kitchen and I see a small crumb on the floor. I'm about to leave the kitchen to go up to my office for an appointment. I have the thought, "Who cares about the stupid crumb? I'll get it later." I start to head up to the office but I remember there's a mantra for this moment. This is an opportunity to get in a repetition. So I stop and say to myself, "**Do it anyway, do it now.**" I pick up the crumb and throw it away.

Now, is that a big deal? Well, it depends how you look at it. It's kind of like asking if one pushup in a workout is really that big of a deal. The answer to the question is: not by itself it isn't a big deal. But when repeated, when you accumulate dozens, then hundreds, then thousands, and literally tens of thousands of repetitions, it becomes a *very* big deal. It becomes a way of being, and that way of being completely changes the way you DO life.

That's a really big deal.

With these repetitions, you have become the person who never puts things off. You've become the person who is massively productive, organized, orderly, on top of things, and traveling through life with lightness of being. You become the person who takes care of business on the spot. Your productivity skyrockets, and so does your attitude, because there's so much lightness-of-being that accompanies *being* the person who has no unfinished business dangling over them.

There's no dead weight of:

> *The bills need to get paid.*
> *The washroom needs to get cleaned.*

I have to return all those emails . . .

All the dead weight of unfinished business is gone.
Use the Mantra, **Do It Anyway, Do It Now** to live powerfully and freely and get things done immediately.

Do It Anyway, Do It Now.

26

If Your Memory Was Better, You'd Realize how Amazing You Are

If Your Memory Was Better, You'd Realize How Amazing You Are. I often say that Mental Mastery or Mental Toughness Training is really about unlearning. It's about unlearning all the "weak sauce" that we've picked up along the way that would have us unnecessarily settle, struggle, or worse, suffer.

One of the things that we've been conditioned to do is to practice paying attention to where we have fallen short in the past, where we are falling short in the present, and to where we might likely fall short in the future.

That thinking comes at the expense of acknowledging our excellence. And there is a lot of practical value in being crystal clear with our excellence.

And it's not limited to just feeling better about yourself. It's about actually BEING better. When I can acknowledge how amazing I am, then it is significantly easier for me to step into my own excellence, activate creative genius and create more miracles faster with less effort.

Practice remembering your greatest-ever performances. In fact, go to the effort of making an actual list of all the miracles and improbabilities you've pulled off in your life. Have that be an ever-growing list. Have that list handy all the time and read it frequently.

Because **If Your Memory Was Better, You'd Realize how Amazing You Are.**

If Your Memory Was Better, You'd Realize how Amazing You Are.

27

The Problem Is the Gift

The Problem Is the Gift. Now there should be an asterisk on that, because it's conditional. The problem will never become the gift unless YOU do the work to have it become a gift.

So, the full version of this mantra is **The Problem Is the Gift—if You'll Have It Be**. Or you could say, the problem *can* be a gift, if you'll turn it into one. And here's what that means.

This mantra has a cousin, a first cousin, maybe even a brother, which goes:

> *"Every set of circumstances can be created from, if viewed masterfully."*

In other words, I can take what I'm experiencing as a problem and turn it into a gift, but I'll only do that if I stop having a problem with the event—if I stop interpreting the event as a problem.

I highly recommend starting that practice with all the tiny, seemingly meaningless complaints that you have. Start paying attention to how many times a day you actually have a problem with something that—when you really look at it—doesn't matter. The pen ran out of ink, you spilled a glass of water on the floor, you nicked yourself shaving, your cell phone is running out of juice. The list goes on and on.

We have so many complaints that when you start to pay attention to them, you'll probably be astonished to realize just how many you have. And if you'll get into the practice of interrupting your complaints and replacing them with a mantra like, **The Problem Is the Gift**, you will literally begin to rewire your brain. You are reprogramming yourself from reacting to life problematically to responding (response-ability) to life circumstances with creativity and enthusiasm (at worst, with curiosity).

You can just leave it at that. You don't have to do anything else. That's a repetition.

You have already altered your state in a powerful way. You have elevated your state from low-grade to, at minimum, neutral and maybe even hopeful—or better yet, enthusiastic.

Additionally, you don't even need to know WHY or HOW the circumstance is or will become a gift at first.

Here's an example that happened in my world recently.

My refrigerator broke a couple months ago and I was complaining about it because I lost a bunch of good steaks in the freezer. I was very upset for about ten seconds. And I'm happy about the fact that it was only ten seconds of disappointment. Years ago, it might have been ten days! As a result of my years of practicing replacing complaints with mantras like this one, it only took me ten seconds to catch myself in my complaint—in my state of dis-ease—to upgrade my experience with the mantra, **The Problem Is the Gift**.

A friend of mine who was visiting town and staying with me walked into the kitchen, heard me say the mantra and asked, "How's this a gift?"

I said, "I don't know yet. But I will have it be a gift by virtue of the way I'm going to respond to this. This will turn into a gift."

And here I am, including it in my book. So that alone has it be a gift. I don't need to know how the event is going to become a gift at the time of the event.

All I want to do with this mantra, **The Problem Is the Gift**, is to interrupt my automatic reaction to life as problematic, and open up the possibility of creating something fantastic. I don't need to know what that gift is in the immediate moment. I just want to interrupt the complaint.

From this event, which moments ago I was interpreting as problematic, I get to create something that would have never occurred to me if it wasn't for the "problem" in the first place.

The Problem Is the Gift.

28

Magic Is All There Is

Magic Is All There Is. There is a slightly longer version of this mantra:

> *Magic is all there is. It is the constant in this equation we call life. The variable is my ability to slow down enough and vibe high enough in order to co-create with that magic.*

My favorite of all psychologists was named Carl Jung. He coined the term *synchronicity*. He was well-versed in Eastern philosophy and human psychology. He noticed that everything in the universe seems to be synchronized. More recently this has been proven by quantum physicists. Everything is instantaneously and inextricably connected across space-time.

Earlier, in the chapter on the mantra, **Everything is Unfolding Exactly as It Should,** I referenced the fact that the universe has been unfolding for fifteen billion years with flawless choreography. I mentioned the magical ratio of particles to antiparticles. Another example is the ratio of helium to hydrogen in stars that go supernova. Again, a perfect magical ratio. And from supernovae, the most cataclysmic events in the cosmos (stars going KABOOM!), arise the heavy elements or building blocks of life like carbon and oxygen. Magic.

In quantum physics there's a term *quantum leap* or *quantum jump.* Some refer to it as an example of quantum weirdness. We can call it magic. It's when an electron in orbit around the nucleus of an atom jumps to a different orbit but *doesn't travel the space between the two orbits.* It is simply in one place in the physical universe in one moment, and in the next moment it is elsewhere—but it didn't travel.

Weird? Or magic?

Let me repeat: **Magic Is All There Is. It's the constant in this equation we call life. The variable is my ability to slow down enough and vibe high enough in order to co-create with it.**

So the mantra **Magic Is All There Is** is an abbreviated version of that, and it serves to remind us to slow down and vibe up. And when we do that, the creation of excellence (or magic) becomes faster, more fun, and significantly more effortless.

Magic Is All There Is.

29

I Respond to All of Life with Gratitude and Enthusiasm

I Respond to All of Life with Gratitude and Enthusiasm. What a great reminder. And it actually reminds me of my favorite quote from one of my favorite teachers in the world, Byron Katie:

> *Until you are able to respond to all of life with enthusiasm, your work is not done.*

I couldn't love that more. And it takes training. A LOT of training. So there's real functional value in this mantra. It's a powerful reminder for me to practice upgrading my low-grade responses to reality, like catching myself when I'm in complaint. Complaint by definition is me struggling against reality, which is a battle I will lose 100 percent of the time.

So if I can catch myself when I'm in complaint even once a minute—and by the way, as I've mentioned elsewhere, some scientists think we are in complaint once every 11 seconds, which means we have no shortage of opportunity for repetitions here—I will accumulate 60 repetitions in an hour of upgrading my interpretations from problematic to inspired, to creating states of awe, which I believe is really our default state.

Gratitude and enthusiasm are two of the most powerful emotional states that exist.

The word *enthusiasm*, as you've probably read in other mantras, is actually from the Greek word *entheos*, which breaks down into the "creator within." Theos = creator. En = inside. Enthusiasm activates all forms of creative genius.

Isn't that great?

The better I feel, the better I am, but only always, and only at everything.

I Respond to All of Life with Gratitude and Enthusiasm.

30

Complaining Is Stupid

Complaining Is Stupid. Complaining by definition is me struggling against reality—which I can do, but that's a battle that I will lose 100 percent of the time. (You'll read that several times throughout this book.) And it's a very popular practice isn't it, this complaining business? We've all learned to experience reality problematically—that's what a complaint is.

I was reading a book by Eckhart Tolle (actually I was *listening* to a book by Eckhart Tolle, which, by the way, is very different from *reading* a book by Eckhart Tolle) and during it, he posed a question that froze me in my tracks:

> *What percentage of your day do you spend in a state of wishing things were different?*

That really floored me, because I got real honest with myself, and the truth is, A LOT! And I don't know if I liked that. In fact, I *know* I don't like that. That spoils a lot of opportunities for me to be in a state of joy or gratitude. And it actually deactivates all creative genius. And that's what I mean by saying **Complaining Is Stupid**, because it deactivates all intelligence centers of the brain. It deactivates creative genius. It doesn't have me be amazing.

Ask yourself:

How and when has complaining ever had you be amazing?

Yeah, I know—the answer is never.

There are only two possible benefits that I'm aware of that come from complaining. One is venting, and I'll get back to why that's silly in a second. The other is social bonding; more specifically, bonding through negativity.

Now, they're *both* dumb, because the expenses far outweigh the benefits. It's just a bad investment of mental energy.

As far as venting goes, what if you practiced not having a problem with the thing that you're complaining about in the first place?

SLOW. THAT. DOWN.

If you practiced strengthening your ability to respond

(response-ability) to life with high-grade interpretations (like The Problem Is the Gift, and many other mantras in this book) there'd be no steam to vent! You wouldn't be experiencing a problem. Nothing to vent.

And with respect to bonding through negativity, that is spreading toxicity. Not cool. There are an infinite number of alternative, healthy ways to bond. Like offering praise, for example.

I'll reiterate again and again—this stuff takes a TON of practice! And it's worth it!

Make the commitment right now to measurably reduce the frequency with which you complain today as compared to yesterday. And do it again tomorrow. And forever on.

Systematically reduce the number of complaints that you generate each day. (And by the way, I'd venture to say that 99 percent of our complaints occur silently in our minds.) And maybe one day, you'll complain no more. And instead of complaining—having a problem with what is—you'll automatically respond to life with grace, creativity, and enthusiasm.

Complaining Is Stupid.

31

If It Ain't Light, It Ain't Right

If It Ain't Light, It Ain't Right. This is a fun one. In all of my years of working with people on human peak performance, I must've asked thousands, maybe even tens of thousands of people to describe to me their peak performances in life.

Do you know that zero of them ever described a peak performance as "weighty" or "heavy" or "problematic" or "stressful" or "worrisome"?

Isn't it cool that as humans, we evolved in such a way that the better we feel, the better we are, but only at everything, and only always? I find that pretty damn comforting.

If It Ain't Light, It Ain't Right. It means that if I'm not experiencing the lightness of being in this moment, I'm not interpreting it properly.

I want to do the work to get above The O-line, to upgrade my interpretation of reality in that moment, so I am feeling lightness of being.

When I'm feeling lightness of being is when I create excellence fast, with the least effort.

If It Ain't Light, It Ain't Right is a light-hearted mantra to remind us to stop taking life so damn seriously!

There's a great saying from Egyptian mythology that I learned from the late, great co-founder of The Chopra Center, Dr. David Simon. It goes something like this:

When you die, the gods weigh your heart against the weight of a feather of a bird. If your heart is lighter than the feather, you are free to experience all the magic of the universe. If, however, your heart is heavier than the feather, you are returned to the Earth to continue to learn to lighten up.

If It Ain't Light, It Ain't Right.

32

This Is the Best Damn Thing That Could Have Happened

This is the Best Damn Thing That Could Have Happened. What a phenomenal mantra that we can use to tremendously elevate our states in a moment's time.

Recently, my refrigerator broke. (I mentioned this event in The Problem Is the Gift, a related mantra, but it's a fresh story, a relevant one, and it bears repeating.) And it wasn't a big deal. Actually nothing is a big deal—unless you make it one. I wasn't making it a big deal because I caught it in time and nothing had spoiled. I have a spare refrigerator in my garage. So if anything, I may have considered it to be a minor inconvenience. I also have a home warranty company that's very effective. So, no big deal. They came out and they fixed it. I actually enjoyed my time with the repair guy who was a big dude, a huge guy from Poland. We were talking about all kinds of stories. I ended up giving him a copy of *The Daily Dose*, which was really fun. And so it was actually a good time.

Four days later, I woke up, went to the kitchen for a glass of water and found the kitchen floor covered in water. The refrigerator was dead and all the steaks that I loaded up into the freezer were spoiled.

I wasn't so chill this time.

In fact, I went sort of postal. And I may or may not have dropped a whole bunch of creatively crafted F-bomb laced sentences. Rapid-fire. I did that for about ten seconds.

But then I used the ultimate practice which is the most fundamental Mental Toughness Training practice that I know of: Catch, Own and Replace.

I caught myself feeling angry.

Then I owned it by saying, "I'm not angry because the refrigerator broke again. I'm not angry because I think my home warranty company took the cheap way out instead of replacing the fridge by trying to fix it. I'm not angry because that nice man obviously did a terrible job of diagnosing the problem and correcting it. I'm not angry because all the food spoiled. I'm not angry because I have to clean up all the water. I'm angry because I'm thinking like a scrub right now."

And then I replaced my low-grade thinking with two mantras.

The first one was the ultimate neutralizer mantra, which we talked about earlier: Ain't Bad, Just Is.

I interrupted my internal tirade by saying to myself—AND MEANING IT—"Ain't Bad, Just Is."

In that one moment in time, it stopped being a problem for me that the refrigerator broke AGAIN, and that this time all the food (expensive steaks included) had spoiled. It just stopped being a problem. How powerful is that?!

So I neutralized the circumstance such that it became simple data, like "Today is a Wednesday." Just is. No highs about that. No lows. Just is.

All the food is spoiled and must be thrown away. That's just information. No plus or minus, no charge either way. No problem, no anger, no enthusiasm. That was my first replacement: Ain't Bad, Just Is.

But I didn't stop there. I decided I'd prefer to feel even better than neutral.

So I further upgraded my state by busting out with, **This Is the Best Damn Thing That Could Have**

Happened, and I had *that* be true.

And that's the real takeaway that I want you to have for this mantra. You can choose to have that actually be true. **This Is the Best Damn Thing that Could Have Happened.**

That can be your truth. Now, if someone was there and they heard me say, "This is the best damn thing that could have happened," they might say in response, "What are you talking about, man? How's that? That's a huge mess to clean up. That water could damage your wood floor. And all these steaks—*expensive* food—it's all spoiled! And now you're without a refrigerator again. How do you figure that's the best damn thing that could have happened?"

My response would have been, "I don't know yet. Give it a minute. But I know it will be, because I'm going to create something excellent out of this. By virtue of the way that I am choosing to interpret and respond to this, it will become **the Best Damn Thing that Could Have Happened.**

**This Is the Best Damn Thing that
Could Have Happened**

33

Fun Is the Most Responsible Thing You Can Do

Fun Is the Most Responsible Thing You Can Do. I love that I have spent my entire career examining human peak performance. Because it's fun! And a huge part of why it's so damn fun is because it's true that as human beings we're at our best when we feel our best.

For over a quarter of a century, I have been interviewing people from all walks of life on the question of "What were your best ever lifetime performances?" in anything—sports, music, dance, public speaking . . . anything. I must have asked tens of thousands of people that question. And I followed it with: "When you were in the zone, when you were really crushing it, when you were having those peak performances, how did that feel?"

Not one human has ever responded with a descriptor that's even remotely negative. Everyone describes peak experiences as characterized in some way by lightness of being. There's an entire book, entitled *Flow*, written on the subject.

In the book, author Mihaly Csikszentmihalyi talks about a characteristic of the flow state, which equals the zone, which equals peak performance, and it is the experience of intrinsic reward. I interpret that to mean, simply, *having fun*.

I actually have a lot of fun making fun of that old neurotic, dumb phrase:

There's a time for work and a time for play.

That's one of the dumbest statements I've ever heard, because it's infinitely incongruent with every shred of human peak performance research that's ever been conducted.

No one has ever described peak performance as a damn struggle.

So, really? There's a time for not having fun? Wrong. All there is is time for fun.

Fun is the most responsible thing you can do.

34

I Wish I Wasn't Wishing Shit Was Different

I Wish I Wasn't Wishing Shit Was Different.

See what I did there?

It's funny, but it's also very legit.

Let's put it into question form.

What percentage of your day do you think (if you get real honest with yourself) you spend in a state of "wishing things were different"?

Don't even get into justifying that they should be different, or if they shouldn't be different; I'm just asking:

How much of your waking conscious time do you spend in a state of dis-ease?

How much time do you spend being uncool with what is, and struggling against reality?

As I mentioned earlier in the **Complaining Is Stupid** chapter, Eckhart Tolle, the author of the great books, *The Power of Now* and *A New Earth*, posed this question, and it stopped me in my tracks. This was probably a decade ago, and I've never forgotten my answer. My first answer remains the same: A LOT.

I'm a lot better at it now than I was ten years ago when I first heard the question. It's because of practice—the practice of replacing complaints with expressions of genuine gratitude and enthusiasm.

I always laugh when I see those old-school bumper stickers that say things like "I'd rather be fishing" or, "I'd rather be on my boat" or, "I'd rather be golfing."

I've always joked with the idea of creating bumper stickers like:

> *I'd rather stop wishing I was somewhere else.*
>
> *I wish I wasn't wishing shit was different.*

Practice being the person who lives by what Byron Katie's greatest book is called: *Loving What Is.*

I Wish I Wasn't Wishing Shit Was Different.

I am practicing loving what is, because when I am able to love what is, what is is what I want.

I Wish I Wasn't Wishing Shit Was Different.

35

Worry Is a Misuse of Imagination

Worry Is a Misuse of Imagination. Worrying IS imagining. More specifically, worrying is imagining a problematic future. Worrying is imagining what you don't want to have happen. And it's even worse than that. Worrying is imagining what you don't want to have happen and also believing that when it happens, your life will be worse. Ew. How crappy is that?!

And we do it ALL DAY LONG!

Why do we worry so much? You know the answer. Because we have learned to. And the great news? We can UNLEARN. Unlearning is central to Mental Toughness. We can raise our awareness to all the times throughout the day when we feel the anxiety that immediately accompanies thoughts of what could "go wrong" (as if everything isn't unfolding exactly as it should). And then we can immediately replace them with this mantra— **Worry Is a Misuse of Imagination**—AND follow it up with another mantra . . . Like, "Ain't Bad—Just Is" or "Best Damn Thing That Could've Happened" or "I Create Excellence from All Circumstances."

In the Visualize Perfection chapter, we discuss just how powerful the images we fill our minds with can be. What we think about, we bring about. Said another way, thoughts become things.

That's a superpower! Filling our minds with images generated by worry is just plain unintelligent. There may be some value in briefly considering what we *don't* want in order to help clarify what we *do* want.

But it is abundantly clear that whatever we focus upon, we are creating. So why focus on worry?

Worry Is a Misuse of Imagination.

36

Pain Is Inevitable, Suffering Is Optional

Pain Is Inevitable, Suffering Is Optional. There's a huge distinction in this mantra—the difference between pain and suffering. There's nothing wrong with pain. Pain is a part of the human experience. It gives us contrast. Pain like sadness, for example. I actually think it's sweet.

Sadness is a sweet experience that I get to have. And, of course, I don't have to ONLY have sadness. But sadness gives contrast to joy, and that's what makes it significant.

If there was no darkness, there would be no such thing as light. If there was no nighttime, there'd be no such thing as daytime. It would only be time.

The psychologist Carl Jung used to define health as the perfect balance of opposites. And he relied on the imagery of the Yin-Yang symbol, which beautifully represents the balance of opposites, the dark and the light, the anima and the animus, introversion and extroversion, etc.

Suffering occurs when I judge my pain as problematic. "Oh, I can't believe this is happening to me. I wish this was over. I wish I wasn't feeling this sadness."

With those thoughts I have now polluted the pain. By itself, pain can be beautiful. Certain ancient philosophies support that everything, when experienced fully, becomes joy.

So if I can let myself simply experience sadness, the pain of sadness or sorrow, there is no problem in that. It's simply, without any judgment, an experience.

But when I start to judge it by saying, "I wish I wasn't feeling this way, I wish this wasn't happening," then I have desecrated the beauty of an opportunity to experience the pain of sadness as it is, in its simplicity.

So pain is inevitable—an inevitable element of life. And thank God for that.

Suffering, however, is optional, which means we can opt out of it.

That is what Buddha dedicated his entire life to: the

examination of whether it was possible to live free from suffering.

And my understanding of his life's work is that, yeah, it is in fact possible.

So pain is inevitable. Thank God for that.

Suffering however, is optional. Let's not choose it.

Pain Is Inevitable, Suffering Is Optional.

37

Move the Doubt Right Out

Move the Doubt Right Out. I am absolutely of the belief that when we come into this life, we are purely doubtless. In fact, what does the act of doubting even mean? It means *the behavior of entertaining the possibility of not getting what you want.*

That's what doubting is. Entertaining the possibility of not having, being, doing, or getting what you want.

When we come into this life, we haven't had any experiences that could be labeled "failure." Yet. We don't even know what "failure" means, this concept of something going "wrong." Yet.

When we come into life, we are experiencing reality as a field of infinite possibilities. We aren't even wondering if something that we want is available or not. We haven't been taught to do that. Yet. We don't have that kind of curiosity. We simply exist within the state of pure abundance. That's our natural state until we are well-educated about our limitations.

I talk a lot about the ALL IN! state—the infinitely committed state—which we are in most of the time. And the nature of that state, what makes it so powerful, is that when we are in it, we're not entertaining the possibility of failure.

When I'm ALL IN! or infinitely committed, I'm doubt-free. I'm too busy doing what it takes to accomplish the mission to entertain "failure." Even if it's just going to the store to pick up a loaf of bread so I can make a sandwich for lunch. When I'm ALL IN! I'm not entertaining or worrying about all the possible things that could go wrong. I'm simply doing what it takes to accomplish the task.

But interestingly, the human experience has so many paradoxes. One of them is that when I'm engaging in the behaviors that are actually, truly, very important to me, I bring in doubt. I bring all kinds of doubt into the equation.

Suppose that your big mission is that you want to start your own business. You want to be an entrepreneur. And then, as soon as that thought occurs, the immediate next thought is,

Move the Doubt Right Out

Well, how's that going to work?

For most of us, that's not a question born out of curiosity. It's much more often a question born out of doubt.

Are you going to be able to . . . ?

How are you going to get the money?

How's this going to work?

Are you even qualified?

What do you know about running a business?

. . . and blah, blah, blah.

We bring doubt into the equation.

But we don't need to. In fact, not only do we not need to bring in doubt; doubt is dead weight.

So when I have a great idea, some fantastic mission, I want to pay very close attention to my thinking.

You've heard me say it before in the description of many other mantras:

I want to live in a state of perpetual self-inquiry, always asking myself questions, catching myself when I'm feeling unpleasant.

So when I'm feeling doubtful, I want to catch that, and use this mantra.

Move the Doubt Right Out.

Remember that your natural state is certainty, doubtlessness or knowing. K N O W I N G ! ! !

Move the Doubt Right Out, because it's not welcome.

Move the Doubt Right Out.

38

#BDDOML

#BDDOML is my first hashtag mantra, and it stands for Best Damn Day of My Life.

It's not a euphemism—it's a declaration.

I started a ritual about two years ago. As soon as I wake up, my first action step is to make the declaration that *this is the best damn day of my life.*

Instead of waiting to see if great things happen, I simply initiate the day by having it be legitimately true for me, that this, by virtue of my decision-making, is in fact the best day of my life. Why not? Why would I not do that?

Why would I create any contingencies and then wait for something to occur in order to simply decide that this is the best damn day of my life?

Well, I never came up with a legitimate reason to wait. And in fact, not only did I not come up with a reason to wait, I discovered that when I bring that high vibrational state—which is characterized by enthusiasm and inspiration and gratitude and intrigue and awe—when I bring all those high-grade states into my day right out of the gate, I end up creating better days. I end up creating more excellence, faster and with less effort.

So whenever someone asks me, "Hey, CD, how you doing?" I use that inquiry, in that very moment, as a reminder to make the declaration again. **#BDDDOML**.

But I don't wait for anybody to ask me the question, "how are you today?" I start the day that way. There are some days (rarely) in which I'll never talk to one person. I still make the declaration.

I'm not going to wait. As soon as I wake up, I make the declaration on my own.

And later, if anyone in the world should happen to ask me, "How are you?" I say, "Thank you for asking. This is the best damn day of my life." And what I mean is "Thank you for the reminder to redeclare, because I may have forgotten that this is the best damn day of my life." Maybe I'd fallen out of "the best day of my life" state, and their question reminded me of where I want to be.

Sometimes I get interesting responses to that. Let's

say I'm at the grocery store and the checkout person asks me how I'm doing, and I say my answer, #BDDOML, they might say, "Wow. Really? Why? What happened?"

And I'll say, "I woke and I decided that it's the best day of my life. That's what happened. I decided it first thing this morning, and then because you asked me right now how I'm doing, I've decided it again."

I don't want to wait to see how anything goes in the outer world in order to elevate the inner world.

I have the freedom and the ability to use my mind in such a way that I get to actually legitimately believe that this is the best damn day of my life. So I'm doing that.

Some people hear it, some people don't. I don't care.

Now I will say this: some days it ain't so easy. I wake up, and for whatever combination of reasons, I'm not really feeling like this is the best day of my life. Especially if I'm sick.

To me, that's the hardest time—when I'm feeling ill—to actually have #BDDOML be true. And that is some of the greatest inner world work I could ever do. Despite the challenge, despite the circumstance, to still power through intentionally and choose that this is, in fact, the best damn day of my life—that work pays off.

Since starting this ritual about two years ago, I have missed zero days. I have had many, many days where I felt like saying,

> *"Oh, the hell with it, for God's sake! What's the big damn deal, CD? It's just another day, who cares?"*

But then I follow that with

> *"No, man. Don't bail on this. Elevate. It's going to pay off tremendously."*

Even if you're sick and even if you feel like crap, do the work and that work always pays off.

Best damn day of my life. It's a brilliant choice. I encourage you to make it every day.

#BDDOML

39

Is It True? Is It Necessary? Is It Kind?

Is It True? Is It Necessary? Is It Kind? The power of the conditioning of our past is so strong that it governs our thinking and therefore also our language. And with our language, we create our lives. And with our language, we can also change another's life—in an instant. Our language could bring either massive joy or massive hurt to someone else.

This mantra can serve as a filter for our language. Three questions. **Is It True? Is It Necessary? Is It Kind?** The way it works is that if the comment I am about to make doesn't satisfy each of the three questions—with a yes, of course—then I don't utter it.

I KNOW!!! I had the same exact response when I first heard this one. I thought to myself, "Well, hell. If everything I ever say from now on must be true, necessary AND kind, I'll be mute!!!"

Ha!

Let's not be rigid with these filters. Let's let the mantra, **Is It True? Is It Necessary? Is It Kind?** serve as a gentle guide to help us upgrade the quality of our commentary. If I am willing to simply have the three-part inquiry open in my mind—with light-heartedness—over time, I will become much more conscious, purposeful and intentional with what I choose to articulate to the world.

And that is what Mental Toughness Training is about: strengthening my mind (over time) so that I can be conscious, intentional, purposeful. And thus live powerfully.

Let's open up each of the three filters/questions.

Is It True?

It's amazing how much of what we say is NOT true! It's not necessarily that we're lying. It's just that what we think is true so often isn't. Be amused by that, please. Because it really is funny if you see it the right way. Our beliefs govern us. Completely. When I am articulating a thought, my language is reflective of whatever belief I am entertaining in that moment. When you start to really pay attention to what's coming out of your mouth, you might be surprised that every once in while you make a statement that isn't even true. Just moments ago, I went to ask the office at the condominium complex where I'm staying this week if they could print out a return label for an incorrect item I received from Amazon. They asked if it was UPS or USPS, because the UPS guy already came and went for the day. I confidently asserted that it was being picked up by USPS. Then I went back to the email thread and discovered it is, in fact, UPS. I was completely wrong. Did I lie to them? No. Did I believe I was right? Yes. Was what I said true? No. I did NOT ask myself if it was true before uttering, "USPS!" I did, however, ask myself moments later, discover the truth and correct my action. So, it can work retroactively as well!

Is It Necessary?

What a great question. Open up this inquiry for yourself today. How much of what I say is really necessary? Another way of inquiring would be to ask, "Who is the benefactor of this comment?" That can be eye-opening. Am I about to make a statement because I am seeking recognition? Am I about to make a comment that is gossipy? Am I about to make a comment that only serves to win an argument? Less is more here. It reminds me of a great quote, "Still waters run deep."

Is It Kind?

Let's operationalize the term "kind" as it appears in this third question. I doubt any of us needs it pointed out that saying mean or spiteful things isn't helpful. But does **Is It Kind?** mean that I should only ever say things that are sweet and unoffensive? HELL NO! There's a comment (that does satisfy all three filters) that I express very often in conversations with my private coaching client prospects. When we are discussing the possibility of working together, I tell them, "I will not avoid offending you in the name of serving you." My serving them is why we would work together in the first place, and there is no service in avoiding the truth. Or even softening it. Yes, I want to put effort into using language that is more likely to be heard effectively, but I do not want the term "kind" to influence me to protect people from taking offense. We have all been conditioned to manage other people's impressions and opinions of us—as if that's important or skillful. I love the Byron Katie quote, "Your opinions of me are none of my business."

So, in this context, "kind" could very well mean courageous. Courageous enough to speak transparently when the outcome could quite possibly involve the listener taking offense. Serving others is the highest expression of kindness.

Is It True? Is It Necessary? Is It Kind?

40

EnLIGHTen Up!

EnLIGHTen Up! The root word is "light."

Light. In the thirty-year span of my career, whenever I have asked anyone to describe their peak performances, no one has ever chosen to describe them as weighted down with pain, struggle, frustration, nervousness or disappointment.

In fact, it's quite the opposite. They almost always use terms like light or effortless.

So there's great incentive for us to shed the dead weight of unnecessary anxiety and unnecessary frustration and all the other low-grade states that we choose to think our way into.

I had a friend once who really got frustrated when I would tell him to lighten up. He was a rather intense individual. He really took it quite personally when I said, "Hey, man, just lighten up." He actually hated it.

Me? I love the reminder, quite honestly. When

155

someone says to me, "Hey, lighten up!" that's a beautiful reminder for me that maybe I am, in that moment, choosing to interpret reality in a pretty poor way.

So I want to just say thank you. It's a great reminder for me to choose to ascend way above The O-Line. In other words, to upgrade the heck out of my interpretations of reality in that moment, so I shed the dead weight of complaint. And instead I can activate states like gratitude, awe, inspiration, enthusiasm . . . which are the "on" switches for all intelligence centers of the brain, which make it easy for me to create excellence faster, and with less effort.

EnLIGHTen Up!

41

Open to Miracles, Cool with what Happens

Open to Miracles, Cool With What Happens. This is actually a fun and very slightly abbreviated way of saying the other version of this mantra, which happens to be one of my favorite definitions of enlightenment:

Having a mind that is open to everything.
And attached to nothing.

What it means is that I'm simultaneously completely open to the possibility of co-creating miracles every moment of my life, while also being perfectly cool with whatever I get.

Now that second part, being cool with what happens—that's Mental Toughness. That's actually a prerequisite for Mental Toughness. In certain Eastern philosophies, they call that non-attachment, or being blissfully detached from outcome.

I always want to stay open to the possibility of creating miracles. After all, for goodness' sakes, you are a miracle!

If you do the math on you (which has been done) the bottom line is that you're an incomprehensible improbability, which equals a *miracle*. So why would you ever not be in the expectation that you are going to create miracles all day long?

And, since I have an ego that doesn't always conform with the way the universe feels like stuff needs to go down, I also want to practice embracing everything, knowing that I can create from it. Every set of circumstances can be created from, if viewed masterfully.

I want to view whatever happens masterfully, so I'm expecting miracles, and I'm totally cool with what happens, because I know I can't lose. If I get what I want, I celebrate; when I don't, I get to grow.

Open to Miracles, Cool with what Happens.

42

Sometimes the Fastest Way to Get There Is to Slow Down

Sometimes the Fastest Way to Get There Is to Slow Down. It's one of my favorite paradoxes in life—and life is full of paradoxes.

Slowing down is one of the most powerful disciplines I've ever incorporated into my life.

Slowing down is absolutely *the* most lucrative discipline I've ever incorporated into my life.

Slowing down is such a profound practice. Slowing down speaking, slowing down thinking, slowing down responding—that's a good practice.

When people ask you a question as simple as, "Hey, how are you doing today?" Slow it down. Don't just blurt out. "Good, good, fine. Hanging in there." Slow down as if they'd asked you "What'd you have for dinner yesterday?"

How are you? "Yeah, I'm a little frustrated." or, "I'm

good." (Or, **#BDDOML!**)

Slow it down. Slow down your walking. Slow down your eating. I don't slow down driving—I like driving fast—but pretty much everything else I've slowed down.

I mentioned slowing down—the practice—is the most lucrative practice. And I mean that. It's amazing! I have seriously accelerated the rate at which I create wealth by slowing down.

Slowing down more specifically to be in more service to people that could use my gifts and my offering.

Slowing down to listen more deeply to what people are saying.

Slowing down to listen more deeply to what people are *not* saying.

Slowing down to study people to see how I might be of service to them.

Slowing down to ask focused questions with the singular intent of really understanding, more deeply, a person's experience, to see if there's a way that I could serve them, perhaps in a way that's bigger than they're even asking for, because they don't know what to ask for.

Slowing down and responding to all life . . . with

curiosity. Always being in inquiry. "I wonder if the next person whose path I cross today could perhaps use my service.

Slowing down to listen to the person who's speaking to you as if they are the most important person in the world.

Slowing down to really experience what's going on in the midst of chaos. I could go on and on, but I'm in a hurry to finish writing this book—ha! Kidding.

Practice finding opportunities today to experiment with the discipline of slowing down.

Sometimes the Fastest Way to Get There Is to Slow Down.

43

When We Choose Enthusiasm the World Opens Up for Us

When We Choose Enthusiasm the World Opens Ip for Us. It's true!

Enthusiasm is one of the most intelligent states that we could ever choose to think our way into. The word enthusiasm itself comes from the Greek word, *entheos*, which means the creator within.

So when I choose to think my way into enthusiasm, I'm activating creative genius. And therefore I am much more capable of co-creating excellence.

The mantra says *the world opens up for us.* The world is really always totally opened up for us. What varies from moment to moment is my ability to co-create with it based on my state.

So when I'm having a problem with reality, well, I'll lose that battle . . . but only a hundred percent of the time!

When I choose to elevate my state, the possibilities

that are already available to me become apparent.

Several years ago I was taking a trip to give a talk in San Francisco. I was flying from Phoenix to San Fran on the same day as the talk, which was a very unusual circumstance, but it's what the company decided. That decision is a little risky because there's a long list of circumstances that could occur that would actually have me not show up on time. And several of those exact circumstances actually occurred.

Long story short is I'm on the plane. We had gone out onto the tarmac. We had been delayed, delayed again and delayed again. The flight was delayed before we even got on the plane to get on the tarmac to get delayed again. And then there was a mechanical problem. We had to go back to the gate. When we got back to the gate, the captain came on the intercom and said the flight crew had timed out. So the flight was now canceled, after all that.

At that point, people started going berserk.

One guy in particular was standing in the aisle, on the phone with a ticket agent from the airline. And he was going postal! He was right next to me.

And I must admit, it's sort of funny: I was on my way

to give a talk on Mental Toughness and I was WAY below the O-Line, thinking, "Oh my God, what happens now? I'm not gonna make it. This is horrible. I can't believe it. Do I just send them back their money? I've never had this happen before. I hate this. Oh, my God!"

I was going down, down, down until I saw this guy who was way further below the O-Line than I was. He was screaming, literally screaming, at this woman on the phone. I looked at him and I thought, "Oh, this is a great reminder of how I don't want to be. I'm going to go the other direction from this gentleman."

And I *decided* to vibe way up, and I literally created enthusiasm. I actually did the work. It only took a few seconds, but they were unbelievably valuable, life-altering seconds.

I changed my thinking from, "This is a problem!" to, "This is amazing. This is going to be incredible. I'm going to create excellence out of this. I'm going to have a great story about this!" (Which I'm in the middle of telling you right now.)

I profoundly (and rapidly) altered my emotional state. I *literally* created enthusiasm. I didn't fake it. You can't do that. I literally got excited about what I could potentially create from this exact set of circumstances.

Then I called the airline from that elevated state. When the woman answered, I very enthusiastically said, "Hey, Diane! This is amazing! You and I are in a game, we're in the middle of creating a miracle. We're going to do that together! Are you down?"

And she said, "This is incredible. I never get calls like this."

I'm like, "I know! Let's do it!"

Fast forward a little bit. Diane guided me to a gate a ways down the terminal where there was a plane that was also going to San Francisco, but which had been slightly delayed. She didn't even know if the plane had left yet or not.

She told me to run. "Hurry, get to gate A9! Is the door open?"

"Yeah the door's open!"

"Ask the guy to not shut the door! And ask if there are any seats left!"

And I asked the gate agent if there were any seats left.

And he said, "No . . . um, wait, wait. Oh, yes. As a matter of fact there is one seat left," and he gave it to me.

Of all the passengers on that canceled flight I was on, why didn't anyone else create that opportunity?

I got the last seat because I chose enthusiasm.

The solution was there for everyone, but the person who chose enthusiasm was the one who accessed it.

Choose enthusiasm more and more each day, and observe how the world opens up for you.

**When We Choose Enthusiasm the
World Opens Up for Us.**

44

You Can't Create from a Low-Grade State

You Can't Create from a Low-Grade State. Maybe you can, but you can't create much, and you're not going to create anything great in a sustainable way, that's for sure. What you *will* create from a low-grade state is chaos.

When we choose to interpret reality in a way that has us feel unpleasant, we are literally deactivating all forms of creative genius within us, all forms of intelligence whatsoever.

When I'm in low-grade states like frustration, anxiety, or disappointment, I could maybe create a little bit of goodness. But if I'm in a panic state, I can only create survival. That's good, right? Survival is good. If I'm going into a panic state, I'm thinking thoughts like, "Oh my God, I could die!" and I release adrenaline, which will have me, for example, be physically stronger

167

in that moment, and that helps me survive whatever threat is present.

But how often is it that we're in situations where we're legitimately concerned about our actual physical survival? It's hopefully very rare for you.

If you're in the military, or if you're a first responder, you are fully aware of the importance of controlling states amidst chaos and real threat!

But most of us who aren't voluntarily putting ourselves into threatening situations still create panic responses to everyday events. And it's not useful.

When I'm thinking thoughts like, "Oh my God, I could be screwed. Oh my God, this is bad, this is really bad!" I'm releasing the chemicals that are good for survival, but not for creativity.

So pay attention. One of the most fundamental practices of all Mental Toughness Training that is really central to almost every one of these mantras is the ability to self-inquire and catch yourself when you are in a low-grade state. What a monumental skill it is to be able to catch yourself when you have thought your way into a low-grade state, and then go to the effort of changing your thinking. Turning it around and creating a high grade state, like one of enthusiasm, gratitude, inspiration, awe, competency, joy, love, compassion—the states that have us be amazing. The states that have it be easier and faster to create excellence.

And, once again, it takes a ton of practice. Hence all these mantras to help us!

You Can't Create From A Low-Grade State.

45

Doubt the Doubt

Doubt the Doubt. If you have a doubt, then doubt the doubt. I've stolen this one from Maharishi Mahesh Yogi, or at least I think so. He was the guru for the Beatles.

When they hired him to be their personal guru they really normalized transcendental meditation. When you practice transcendental meditation, or TM, what you're doing is stopping going to the effort of caring about your thoughts and instead letting your mind slow down enough so that maybe on occasion you have a space between your thoughts. And when you're having no thought you can't actually have any doubt.

Doubt is a skill. Yeah, that's interesting. Isn't it? Let's look at this idea.

When we come into this life, we are purely doubtless. How could we have doubts? We don't even know what doubt is. What is doubt? If you're going to explain to someone what doubt is, what would you say? If they asked you, "Hey, can you please explain doubt to me? Can you teach me how to doubt? I don't think I doubt enough." How would you tell them to do that better?

How does someone actually doubt?

Doubt is the act of entertaining catastrophic future thinking. Okay, maybe not catastrophic, but it is low-grade future thinking.

Doubt is entertaining the possibility of not having, being, doing or getting what you want at some point in the future, whether that's a second from now, or an hour or two, or ten years from now.

We don't know how to doubt when we come into life. When we start life, we are purely doubtless. Isn't that interesting? We have had no experience of not getting what we want. So how could we doubt getting something? We have had no repetitions of entertaining the possibility of the universe *not* having what we want, or us not being able to create what we want.

We started accumulating repetitions early on in life, however. We've accumulated so many repetitions of entertaining the possibility of not having, being, doing or getting what we want. And we have therefore mastered doubt.

So the mantra here is to undo doubt.

Imagine, visualize for a moment, the you who has eliminated doubting as a behavior from your life. Do that.

It's hard to do. It's worth the effort, though.

Give it a sec. Visualize the you, the adult you, now, who after concerted effort of practicing doubting the doubt, has freed themselves completely from doubt . . .

Who are you then?

What are you like?

What do you do with your mind, with the time that you formerly used to entertain the possibility of not getting what you want?

Well, I might argue that you're using that time to create. So now all you ever do is use your cognitive time to create.

So, here's the practice.

Catch yourself when you're doubting yourself— when you're doubting whether or not you're able to create what it is that you want.

And then know, in that moment, that that behavior

has been learned. You're simply rehearsing something you learned. So doubt that lesson when you have a doubt.

Doubt the Doubt.

46

Get Your Head Outta "Yeah, But"

Get Your Head Outta "Yeah, But." It's obviously a fun play on words here. And it's every bit as poignant as it is playful. An interesting phenomenon, one that we all experience immediately after the arising of some great idea, is that our minds follow that idea with "Yeah, but" thinking. Immediately!

Let's take an example. Since I do a lot of work with high-performing sales teams, I'll use a real-life example from that world. A heavy-quota-carrying sales rep decides that she's gonna knock it out of the park and have her best quarter ever. The millisecond in time after she tells herself, sincerely and authentically, that she's gonna have the best quarter of her career, her brain generates thoughts like, "Yeah, but how the hell are you going to beat last quarter?" Or "Yeah, but the pandemic." Or "Yeah, but the tech industry is getting hammered right now." And a ton of other fear-based, obstacle-natured thoughts. These weak, intelligence-deactivating thoughts occur IMMEDIATELY and without invitation. Why? Because we have been conditioned to practice having them. And we don't even know it.

Think about the eleven-year-old you who shared the idea that you wanted to be an astronaut and the President of The United States and an actress and a pirate. And upon sharing that wonderful, imagination-filled and inspiration-filled fantasy you were informed by the person you shared it with, "Pffft. Yeah, that's cute, but you can't be all of that! That's ridiculous." Your vision was responded to with "Yeah, but . . ." And that happened hundreds of times over the years, so you learned to do it to yourself. Great idea instantly followed by, "Yeah, but . . ."

So this mantra serves as a re-MIND-er to catch yourself when your head is all up in "Yeah, but," and to replace the doubt with enthusiasm and commitment.

Practice being on guard for the "Yeah, but" when you're brainstorming or goal setting. Fully anticipate the arrival of the "Yeah, buts," and when they arrive, replace them instantly with another mantra like, The "How?" Is In The What, or any other thought like, I only create excellence, or, I create all of my desires with effortless ease!

Get Your Head Outta "Yeah, But" and get your mind back into the infinitely abundant state that it existed in prior to being educated about limitations.

Get Your Head Outta "Yeah, But."

47

Visualize Perfection

Visualize Perfection. There is a question that is one of the most powerful and intelligent questions that we can ask ourselves frequently throughout our days. All our days. That question is this:

"What would *perfect* look like here?"

When I was working primarily with elite competitive golfers on strengthening their mental games, we'd always do A LOT of work on their mental preparation routines. "What would *perfect* look like?" appeared in all the various routines. For example, in The Daily Mental Toughness Training Routine, one of the steps is to visualize yourself performing different tasks that occur often in your world and to see yourself performing them perfectly, in your mind's eye, in vivid detail.

Not "pretty good." Not "well." Not "really, really well."

PERFECTLY.

Why? Because your images become instructions to your unconscious mind *to do whatever it takes to make those images real*. This is why focusing too much on what could go wrong is unintelligent. The fact is, we are always visualizing. Fantasizing . . day-dreaming . . . worrying . . . ruminating. Our minds do not discriminate regarding the quality or nature of the thought. If there's a thought there, or an image of some greatness, the unconscious mind will immediately work to make it real. If it is an image of doom, the mind will work equally effectively to create that.

There has been a ton of fascinating research done on how our bodies respond to our thoughts. One study involved teenagers and leaves from the poisonous lacquer tree. The boys involved—all of whom had had previously documented skin rash reactions to contact with the lacquer tree—were told that they were going to have their left forearms rubbed with those leaves. They were immediately dismayed. They were also told that their right forearms were being rubbed with leaves from the benign elm tree, which they were *not* allergic too. (They were blindfolded, and so couldn't see what which leaves were being rubbed on their arms).

Then—plot twist—experimenters switched the plants. Guess what happened? A significant number of the subjects got the rash on the left forearm—which was rubbed with harmless elm leaves. But those participants were of the belief that their left forearms were being rubbed with the poisonous leaves, and therefore they were imagining the rash. They IMAGINED that rash, and they GOT the rash. The imagining that they didn't even know they were engaging in activated cellular memory and created the reaction. Fascinating, huh?

Something similar happened in reverse with pregnant women who were told they were taking a drug that would stop morning sickness. They were also educated extensively on how this new medicine would work (which got them starting to imagine wellness). The researchers actually gave them syrup of ipecac, a poison that should have *made* them vomit—but a significant number of the women became symptom-free. Not only did they cure themselves of morning sickness, they also neutralized the action of a powerful vomit-inducing substance. All because of the images of wellness they were (unknowingly) creating in their minds!

This power works consciously, too—you can use it

with intention. In golf, The Pre-Shot Routine is the brief period of time before every single shot a golfer executes where they do whatever they can within the rules of the game to get completely prepared—and thus maximize the probability of hitting the perfect shot. Jack Nicklaus, arguably the greatest player in all of history, said, "Before every shot, I would go to the movies." What he meant was that in his mind's eye he'd imagine the ball doing precisely what he wanted it to do in advance of making his swing. **Visualize perfection.**

Also in golf, The Post-Game Routine is where you go get all the learning out of the round so you can accelerate your mastery development. In the corporate world this is often referred to as The Post-Mortem—which is really weird! But it's still super useful. And, you guessed it. Visualizing perfection is one of the steps.

But the uniqueness here is that you're using your mind's eye to execute what I call "imaginary do-overs"—and doing them . . . PERFECTLY! You look back on the performance, identify the moments when you would like to do better, and then do imaginary do-overs visualizing perfection. Our brains store these fantasies in the same way that they store real experience.

So get in the repetitions of filling your mind with "memories" of perfect execution.

I once met an Olympic Gold Medalist in high-diving and she told me a story about her training. At the end of every practice of her life, her coach would have her go over into the bleachers in the natatorium and sit and visualize one hundred PERFECTLY executed dives. Half of the dives that she would imagine were dives that she hadn't even attempted yet. She showed me her gold medal and said to me, "I attribute this gold medal to all the perfect dives that never happened that my mind and body think did."

What we think about, we bring about.

Where attention goes, energy flows.

Thoughts become things.

I want to be very MIND-FULL of what I am envisioning. If my thoughts become instructions to the brain to do whatever it takes to make my images reality, I want to be sending instructions to create PERFECTION!!!

Get into the habit of visualizing perfection in all areas of your life, before, during (when possible), and after you execute. See yourself performing perfectly in different possible scenarios. Send instructions for perfect. Routinely ask—and answer—this brilliant question throughout your daily life: "What would perfect look like here?"

Know that in doing so, you are profoundly accelerating your mastery development and increasing the probability of getting what you want, and being who you want to be, faster.

Visualize Perfection.

48

I Am Blissfully Detached from Outcome

I Am Blissfully Detached from Outcome This mantra is another inherently paradoxical one. The less attached I am to getting what I want, the more likely I am to get it. And there's the paradox.

Let's operationalize "attachment" here. In this context, "attachment" is a bit desperate. At least a bit. It could be completely desperate. The belief that not getting what you want will result in your life being less good is a popular belief. We have all learned it. And that belief is at the core of the desperation, or the attachment, that has us be so uncomfortably needy. And neediness is a repellant to all things good.

The presence of the word "blissfully" in this mantra is great. It totally changes the vibe of the mantra. The power of your clear intention is massive. Your ability to choose knowing as a state when it comes to creating excellence in your life is, by itself, very blissful.

The Dalai Lama once said that worry is useless. I say it's even worse than useless. I say it's destructive and damaging. And it's all learned.

Going back to human peak-performance research and observation, never has anyone described a peak performance as characterized by worry. NEVER. Instead, everyone describes peak performances as characterized by serenity, ease, and fun.

So, the paradox again is that if I am truly committed to creating my desires, then I must also surrender to the possibility that the universe has better ideas for me, and I can thus be simultaneously infinitely committed to my desires AND totally unattached to them becoming reality. That's just damn relaxing, isn't it? Or blissful.

I love using this mantra in circumstances when I'm getting nervous about things not going my way. I only get nervous because I am entertaining the weak thoughts about how I need things to go my way, or my life will suck. Who wouldn't feel nervous (or worse) with that kind of thinking? So, when I remember to say to myself in those circumstances, **I Am Blissfully Detached From Outcome**, I instantly and completely transform. I transform from needy to blissful. And it is then that I am most likely to think well and take masterful action, maximizing the probability of creating greatness. And doing it fast!

I Am Blissfully Detached From Outcome.

49

Do Less Better

Do Less Better. One of the biggest mistakes I made earlier in my career was trying to cram so much into my days, so much content into my workshops, so many huge moments into each coaching session, and so many appointments into my calendar. And, lo and behold, another paradox! Not only did that not have me be more productive and skillful, it did the opposite. It had me struggle. Conversely, every time I have purposefully and deliberately, with thoughtful calculation, reduced my "busyness," I have become measurably more productive. And the quality of what I have produced has also improved drastically. My willingness to trust quality over quantity has paid off magically. And it's SOOOOO much more relaxing!

I coach a lot of fast-moving executives and business leaders who live in the incessant urgency of the harried corporate world. They're stretched, stressed, overwhelmed, and exhausted. That's not a very good combination if what you're looking to create is sustained excellence.

I used to live in that same way when I was a licensed therapist, seeing eight clients a day, back to back to back, with practically no time to reset or refresh. When I look back on that time, I can't even imagine how I could have been very helpful to the last six clients each day!

During the pandemic of 2020-2022, people had to work from home, and everyone started doing Zoom meetings. Back to back to back. And everyone just accepted that as the new normal. I would ask my clients if I could have a look at their calendars. It was mayhem. It gave ME anxiety just looking at these days not only full with meetings all smushed up against each other, but also often overlapping! No time for a psychological reset, not to mention lunch. That is NOT the formula for creative genius or maximum productivity. That's the paradox. The intent was to maximize productivity, so the approach was to jam the day full of meetings. The result: crap productivity, burnout, exhaustion, frustration and even a new phenomenon called "Zoom fatigue!"

Do Less Better is a brilliant re-MIND-er to slow it

all down in order to speed it all up. Slow down a lot of things and a lot of goodness will occur faster and with less effort. Doesn't that sound eerily similar to the peak performance state called "The Zone"?!?! This mantra is the most powerful antidote for the poison of overwhelm.

Do Less Better reminds us to take inventory of our days, to have a good, thorough look, often, at how much we are trying to cram into them. It reminds us to examine what we are believing about the usefulness of busyness.

I have never seen **Do Less Better** not work. That is to say, doing less better always leads to increases in all things good: productivity, restedness, clarity, focus, creativity, endurance, resilience, enthusiasm and profitability.

Do Less Better.

50

See the Magic in the Mundane

See the Magic In The Mundane. Happiness Engineer and Poker Pro, Ali Binazir, calculated the odds of any of us occurring precisely as we are. He stretched his calculations all the way from your parents meeting and you being born back to the time when proto-humans walked the Earth. (You probably remember me talking elsewhere in this book about the relationship between particles and anti-particles at the beginning of the universe, but Binazir doesn't go back that far.) What he discovered was that there is basically a 0% likelihood of any of us "occurring"—existing, coming into being—in the first place.

One might argue that that's the stuff of miracles.

Given this simple yet mind-blowing fact about your very being, what could possibly be "mundane" or dull?

See The Magic In The Mundane re-MINDs us to slow down enough to remember that everything is magical by nature of simply being. Nothing is mundane. We simply forget to experience the magical nature of it all.

In graduate school I had a class on death. In that course, we read about a study that was done with centenarians who were asked the question, "Looking back, what would you do different in life?" One of the most popular responses was, "I'd slow down and appreciate how magical life is without me having to do anything to it."

That was true for the centenarians, and it's true for you and me too.

Magic is everywhere. We just have to see it.

See the Magic In The Mundane.

51

Be Curious

Be Curious There is great intelligence in curiosity. Curiosity opens the mind up to insights, learning and discovery. And it's fun, which we have established is a brilliant and responsible thing to do—have fun.

Over time, we are conditioned to replace curiosity with judgment—particularly low-grade judgment. We rehearse having problems with reality. We get really good at that, become expert complainers, and lose our instinctive curiosity. And when the curiosity goes away, creative genius goes with it.

I always encourage folks to ask themselves two questions as soon as possible after something happens that they didn't want. The questions are, "What's the learning in this?" And, "What greatness can I create from this now?"

That is some real valuable curiosity. Can you see how these two questions can lead rapidly to gold?

So when stuff "goes wrong" (which it doesn't, really—it just goes) **Be Curious** and get the gold.

Be Curious.

52

Don't Wait to Be Great

Don't Wait to Be Great—I've said it before and I'll say it again. The #1 mistake that I have observed people making in the creation of their desires is WAITING! More specifically, unnecessary waiting. Putting unnecessary time, and often painfully enormous amounts of time, in between themselves and what they want. And a huge chunk of what we all want involves who and how we are being. We want greatness. Who doesn't want to be great?! Who doesn't want to be masterful? Who doesn't want to be competent and expert? Who doesn't want to simply feel great? We all want that, of course.

Here are a few of the limiting beliefs we have been conditioned to adopt that completely govern us by having us put all that unnecessary *time* between ourselves and our greatness. We have been taught to believe that we need to be recognized by the outer world in order to feel expert. We've been conditioned to believe that we need to have some form of validation or proof in order to qualify as best-in-class. We need for great things to happen in order to feel great. That's all nonsense. It's a bunch of malarky, I tell ya!

This mantra, **Don't Wait to Be Great**, is a sibling of the mantra **Create The State—Don't Wait**. They both serve to re-MIND us to get conscious of where and when in our lives we are waiting unnecessarily. **Don't Wait To Be Great** is a reMINDer mantra that is specific to not waiting to acknowledge yourself as great—at anything you please! It's also a reMINDer to not wait to FEEL great! We have the ability to think our way into any and every emotional state that exists—in a moment's time. So why wait for anything to be different in the outer world in order to be and feel great?!

Don't Wait To Be Great.

About the Author

Chris Dorris is known as The Mental Toughness Coach. He helps people and organizations close the gap between how their lives and businesses are, and how they want them to be.

Acknowledgments

BIGGIE! (The Bare-chested Internet Guru, aka, The Shirtless Wonder. Known to some as Micah Guller.) You are source of infinite creativity and the enzyme that accelerates all of my creations.

My editor, Chris Nelson, for your editing genius and lightheartedness.

All of my clients, past and present. We crafted so many of these mantras spontaneously in the throes of co-creating miracles.

My Entertrainer, B Dubs (Billy Woodmansee), for having hammered home for years the instruction to create stuff with these damn mantras. First the t-shirts, now the book.

My coaches and mentors, Jim Myers, Dr. William Maxwell, The Admiral (Steve Hardison) and THEE Godfather of Coaching (Steve Chandler) for all the love, belief, support, wisdom and the decades of time saved.

Doc Ali (Dr. Alison Arnold) for being everything.

Everything. Seriously.

My Queens Counterpart. DB (Devon Bandison). Best Fawtha eva. The NY version of me. My semi-monthly housemate. How does someone get to know you so deeply so fast. Cigars could be a part of the answer.

John Deines, #BDE, #noFLDs, for your 11th hour style of creating miracles.

A LONG list of professional friends, colleagues, leaders, champions, advisors who have created so many opportunities for me to do my thing, crushing mantras, sporting t-shirts, creating cultural Mental Toughness nomenclature with so many people across the globe. To name a few, Larry Shurtz, Dave Canham, Jon Legend Hunter, David Earhart, Scott Cravotta, Denise Dresser, Amy Slater, Ed McDonnell, Steve "Whattup Playa" Moroski, David Delnero, Heather Venegas, Grant Wood, Gary Weiss, Vince Temperino, Nick Murphy, Jennifer Lagaly, Kevin Guthrie, Frank "Fillz" Fillman, Arym Diamond, McLure Foote, Prak Bebarta. And a jillion others.

My comrades from the golf world whose collaborations resulted in mantras and lifelong friendships. Tom

Cunningham, Mary Bea Porter-King, Coach Randy Lein, Coach Linda Vollstedt, Jeff "GO BIRDS" "OH NO!" Ritter, Scott "I'm DUN! #Pro" Wright.

Gary, Adam, Trudy, Kanako, Koan and Kona. My Mahler Crew. For ALL the love!

Manisha Koirala for introducing me to The Oneness University and all the beauty (and mantras) that came from that experience.

Linda and Johnpaul. My blood.

Mantras Card Deck

COMING SOON

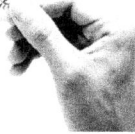

I Can
Choose Peace
Amidst Chaos

Nerves
Can't Exist
In Service

www.christopherdorris.com/mantras-deck

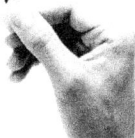

Vibe Up!

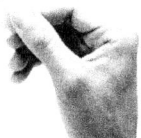

Create The State,
Don't Wait

MENTAL TOUGHNESS CONVOS
START A CONVERSATION!

www.MentalToughnessConvos.com

Come get you some Mental Toughness SWAG! All of these make great gifts, are amazing conversation starters and a fantastic way to effortlessly bring Mental Toughness into your culture.

Ain't Bad - Just Is
www.MentalToughnessConvos.com

Choose Peace Amidst Chaos
www.MentalToughnessConvos.com

I Create From Everything
www.MentalToughnessConvos.com

THERE IS NO "FAILURE" IN MY WORLD
www.MentalToughnessConvos.com

The Daily Dose:

Mental Toughness in 30 Seconds or Less

This started as a daily, morning email. Many of the thousands of people all over the world who get this morning nuggets suggested I should turn them into a book, so I did.

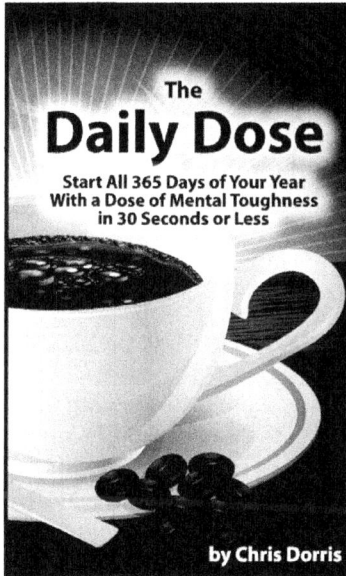

The emails are free and you can get them here:

https://ChristopherDorris.com/dd

The book is available for purchase on Amazon.

Tough Talks:
Conversations on Mental Toughness

At the time of finalizing the editing of this book, there are 105 episodes of my interview-based video podcast!

I've interviewed all sorts of badasses, including:

- Steve Chandler, Thee Godfather of Coaching
- Iyanla Vanzant, Oprah's Coach
- Bob Burg, Author of *The Go-Giver*
- Gary Ridge, CEO of The WD-40 Company
- Manisha Koirala, Author & Bollywood Superstar
- And at least 100 more badasses!

Watch Here: www.ChristopherDorris.com/ToughTalks

ALL IN! 2.0

When you DECIDE—when you're in the ALL IN! state—you activate creative genius, you take masterful and immediate action and you maximize the likelihood of success. Learn what it means to be ALL IN!, learn how to get there, and the 3 step process of using that state to create the life of your dreams.

This is a thorough, robust and "coursified" edition of the original 53-minute ALL IN! audio program - it includes video, quizzes and built-in accountability.

https://christopherdorris.com/all-in-2-0/

Creating Your Dream
– *The Book* –

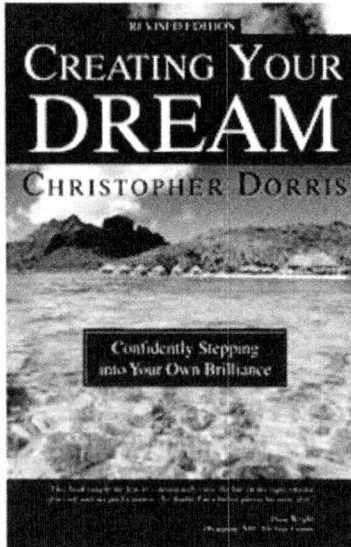

https://christopherdorris.com/shop/

I share my observations from years of training the world's top athletes and executives in the area of peak performance. These are concise and engaging descriptions of the most critical psychological traits-or Mental Toughness Tools-shared by the world's top performers.

I've also included the actual exercises that these peak performers use in their daily Mental Toughness Training regimens.

Creating Your Dream

– The Online Audio Course –

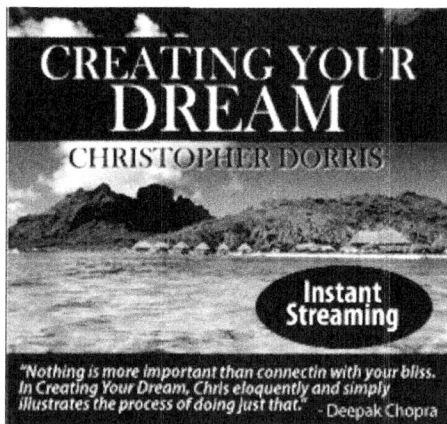

https://christopherdorris.com/shop/

Creating Your Dream takes you through a series of exercises that will help you establish CLARITY on how you ultimately want to use your life, the COURAGE to believe that what you desire is available to you in this abundant universe, and the DISCIPLINE—or Mental Toughness—to do what it takes to make it so.

"Nothing is more important than connecting with your bliss. In Creating Your Dream, Chris eloquently and simply illustrates the process of doing just that."
- *Deepak Chopra*

The Edge:

Mental Toughness For Miraculous Golf

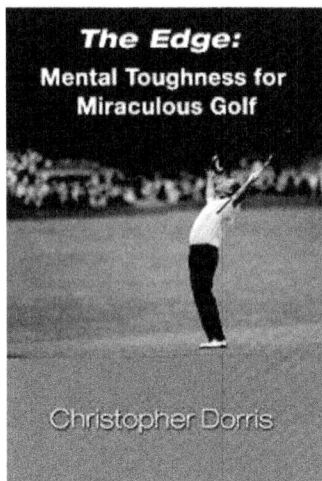

https://christopherdorris.com/shop/

In The Edge, Chris has compiled a collection of his most relied upon Mental Toughness Tools that he uses in his work coaching several of the world's top golfers. It includes a bonus track, The Tips, in which he addresses several of the most frequently asked questions by touring professionals regarding the mental game.

"Chris has been my Mental Coach for years. The Mental Toughness Tools he shares here in The Edge are best in class. You'll find no better product on the Mental Game." - *Michael Allen, PGA and Champions Tour Player, Senior PGA Champion*

Notes

Notes

Printed in Great Britain
by Amazon